Urban Decay

Other books by J. Parry Lewis

BUILDING CYCLES AND BRITAIN'S GROWTH

AN INTRODUCTION TO MATHEMATICS FOR STUDENTS OF
ECONOMICS

URBAN DECAY

An Analysis and a Policy

Franklin Medhurst

and

J. Parry Lewis

with a chapter by Elizabeth Gittus

Macmillan

First published 1969 by
MACMILLAN AND CO LTD
Little Essex Street London WC2
and also at Bombay Calcutta and Madras
Macmillan South Africa (Publishers) Pty Ltd Johannesburg
The Macmillan Company of Australia Pty Ltd Melbourne
The Macmillan Company of Canada Ltd Toronto
Gill and Macmillan Ltd Dublin

Printed in Great Britain by
HAZELL WATSON AND VINEY LTD
Aylesbury, Bucks

Contents

CONTENTS

Foreword

This book gives an account of a methodical investigation into the decay of the fabric and functions of cities and towns. The work has largely been done within the environment of the oldest of all industrial societies, centred in the Lancashire south-east region. In its two hundred years of life a full cycle from invention, innovation, expansion into a period of retraction and decline can historically be recognised.

For many years this cycle, with its sense of inevitability, has been the cause of sober reflection among thoughtful people living in this kind of environment. The Civic Trust in London came into being with the avowed aim of combating this inevitability, and then in 1961 the Civic Trust for the North-West was formed. The Trust's proclaimed task is to seek means by which the North-West of England might become a better place to live and work in. It is committed to a course of action of seeking the best means of extending and deploying our resources for renovation and renewal. In order to do this a number of inquiries and investigations were called for, and one of them was to make a thorough investigation into the problems inherent in the improvement of present twilight areas of the type so widely distributed through the North-West.

The subject of decay of fabric and function was not one, at the time, that seemed likely to commend itself to more orthodox supporters of research, who understandably see research efforts more profitably directed towards greater production and progress, but the Civic Trust of the North-West sees this kind of study as central to its main task. It recognises that the complete rebuilding of an urban environment in Britain was a utopia impossible to achieve, even if desirable, and that much old decaying fabric in our towns would always be part of the urban scene. If this were to be so, then it behoves us to make the best of what we have, and to prolong the life of fabric where we can, in the interests of the best possible use of our construction resources.

A research fund was established in 1962 and accepted by the University of Manchester Institute of Science and Technology to finance a research unit. The fund was available from 1962 until 1966 and was administered by an advisory panel under my chairmanship.

Mr Franklin Medhurst was appointed part-time director of the project. He was then senior lecturer at the University of Manchester Department of Town and Country Planning and a little later the unit was joined by Mr (now Professor) J. Parry Lewis as economics consultant. Together they have been responsible for much of the work and the eventual writing of this book. Mr Michael Eveson became a full-time member of the unit, which was centred in the Department of Building in the Institute. The work was assisted on a number of occasions by temporary appointments of undergraduates from Building, Architecture and Town Planning. The advisory panel recognised from the start the slenderness of the resources that could be deployed in this first research project of its kind. Later the work was to be overtaken in some aspects of its subject by later projects that had teams with more ample resources, but the team and its advisers initiated much thoughtful study and devised research methods that have been freely available to others as time has gone by. One of the inherent problems pervading the work of university teams with little finance, and where much time is freely and generously given, is the problem of completing the publication of the work by draft, redraft, printing and publication. So it has been in this case; but time, in the opinion of the advisory panel, invalidates none of the essential content and the methods by which results have been achieved. A recent publication, *Old Houses into New Homes*, tells of a survey conducted by the Ministry of Housing and Local Government which follows a similar (but more extensive) procedure. The estimates of the condition of our housing stock conforms closely to the estimate subsequently produced by this ministry.

The early parts of the investigation involved the analysis of a particular site within the inner confines of Manchester and required the cordial co-operation of owners and tenants alike, and also a great deal of understanding and help from the local authority. A very considerable amount of information was eventually collected, which after analysis presented clearer pictures of the forces playing on such an area. This information gives some indication of the kinds of controls that might be applied in an effort to extend and improve the condition of both the social environment and the fabric of the buildings. It would, however, be a formidable and ponderous task to enter into this kind of investigation for all areas where deterioration was entering into a state of permanent decline, and much thought came to be devoted to a consideration of a method of examination on a statistical basis of large grid areas of a city, using some of the evidence found in the pilot district. Information of a sufficiently reliable type might, by these means, be obtained in months rather than years, and be pertinent enough for the establishment of priorities concerning the remedial measures—or the demolitions—that might be desirable. These original studies are described in this book, but the present volume is also based on a large amount of further work, stemming from this Civic Trust project, but not financed from it: this further work emanated from the activities of university research units in the Department of Town and Country Planning and the Department of Building and from the corpus of knowledge acquired during the initial project. Further work on various aspects of urban life is proceeding in the university's Centre for Urban and Regional Research, and the lessons learned from our experience in studying decay have helped to mould the approach to urban model building around which much of the research is centred. A practical case study in the Department of Building, financed through the auspices of the Civic Trust for the North-West, concerned with environmental recovery at the new town of Skelmersdale has been under way for the last two years.

There remains a vast amount of work to do if we are to understand all the problems of the causes and effects of urban change. This initial work may help authorities to avoid the worst deterioration and the long-present periods of attrition. Decay by design is much more acceptable than decay by accident. All who have taken part in this project have gained much in their appreciation of towns from it. We would hope that a much more widespread assessment of the nature of decay in our towns and cities will follow.

DENIS HARPER

List of Illustrations

List of Figures

Notes on the Research Project

The project was set up in 1962 to study the conditions and processes of decay, particularly as they can be found in industrial towns. The project was financed by the Civic Trust for the North-West with a grant of £7000.

The work was undertaken by the university by an interdisciplinary team from the departments of Building, Architecture, Town and Country Planning and Economics and work started in June 1962.

The members of the advisory panel and the research group were initially as follows:

Chairman of the advisory panel:	Denis Harper, Professor of Building, University of Manchester.
Director of Research:	Franklin Medhurst, Senior Lecturer in Town and Country Planning, University of Manchester.
Members of the advisory panel:	Laurence Allen, former Town Clerk of Barrow in Furness.
	J. M. Barton, Director of the Civic Trust for the North-West.
	C. F. Carter, Professor of Economics, University of Manchester.
	J. D. R. Francis, Professor of Municipal Engineering, University of Manchester.
	R. H. Kantorowich, Professor of Town and Country Planning, University of Manchester.
	W. Merchant, Professor of Structural Engineering, University of Manchester.
	D. G. Thornley, Reader in Architecture, University of Manchester.
	The Director of Research.

During the course of the research the following changes in the advisory panel occurred; Mr Barton was succeeded by Mr G. Ashworth, both on the panel and as Director of the Civic Trust for the North-West, in July 1965; Professor Carter was succeeded by Mr J. Parry Lewis, then lecturer in Economic Statistics at Manchester University, in January 1963; Professor Francis resigned because of other commitments in March 1964; Professor Merchant died.

Members of the research group:	Franklin Medhurst, Director of Research.
	P. M. Eveson, Senior Research Assistant (full-time), Civic Trust for the North-West.
	J. B. McLoughlin, Lecturer in Town and Country Planning, University of Manchester.
	J. Parry Lewis, Lecturer in Economic Statistics, University of Manchester.

Acknowledgements

The research would have been impossible without the willing co-operation of several hundred occupiers of property in Manchester and of various local-authority officers. It is our hope that this book will make them feel that their efforts were worth while.

The authors wish to pay special tribute to Mr Eveson. Without his energy and enthusiasm, spread over a much longer period than the tenure of his Civic Trust post, this work would certainly not have been completed.

We have also to thank Miss Gittus for her chapter on social aspects of urban decay; Dr Wilmot for processing and examining much of the data; Mr G. C. F. Capper for statistical assistance; and Miss L. Hourani for her invaluable secretarial help throughout the project.

In the final stages of the report-writing Mr John King ably assisted in both the editorial work and in conducting further investigations.

Valuable criticism of the drafts came from several people and especially from Professor Harper and Professor Kantorowich.

Mr Adrian Lovatt assisted in preparing the manuscript and diagrams for the press, and in proof correction and compiling the index.

Parts of Chapter 6 originally appeared in the *District Bank Review*.

CHAPTER 1

The Nature of Urban Decay

In one way or another, at every moment, our towns are changing.
Some grow continuously or in short bursts, some see their population
fall and their buildings become empty or derelict, while others,
possibly appearing to be static, may nevertheless be undergoing
more subtle and gradual changes in land-use, tenure, function or
character. A town is both an arrangement of buildings and spaces
and a location for a community with all its functions and activities.
As the community alters, so may its functions, and these will affect
the uses to which land and buildings are put. Even if, as in the case
of a monastic village, the community and its functions change but
little, the buildings will still tend to change. Weather erodes them,
sometimes beyond repair at reasonable cost, and maintenance may
become selective. If the physical fabric of the town remains almost
unchanged for long, the town becomes a museum piece and attracts
attention of a kind that tends to change the function. New means of
transport alter its accessibility to other towns and encourage people
to visit it to see the characteristics of a previous age. By visiting it
they change it, if only by crowding its streets or making it visitor-
conscious.

Today most British towns manifest change in at least three ways.
They are seen to be growing in size (provided one is allowed to
include growth that may be outside local-government boundaries),
to have more vehicles passing along their streets, and (unless they
have recently taken action about it) to have increasing numbers of
properties that look as if they will soon have to be knocked down. It
was an awareness of this third manifestation of change that prompted
this study, but the more we studied it the more we became aware of
its close links with the other aspects. Be it defined in terms of the
physical condition of buildings, of the quality of environment or of
the state of a culture or civilisation, decay has to be related to change.

It is a natural phenomenon that man can to some extent control or arrest. To prevent it, or to halt its progress, may be possible only through a kind of fossilisation or major surgery. The very word 'decay' is one that conjures up a multitude of unpleasant images, and writers about towns have used it to describe very many different states of affairs, having little in common except some implication of an undesirable change. Sometimes the emphasis is on the physical decay of buildings. At other times it is on the declining attractiveness of the environment, the disappearance of activity, the growth of 'undesirable' activity or even the quality of its administration.

It may very well be that these differing kinds of decay are in some way related, and later in this book we shall produce some evidence against which this supposition may be tested, but we begin by concentrating on the physical decay of buildings. We shall see that although this is sometimes the simple and inevitable result of ageing, it is sometimes brought about unwittingly by short-sighted policies. We shall also see how this decay may have both desirable and undesirable consequences, and how it must be looked upon as but one aspect of urban change, due to both natural and unnatural forces. By understanding it we can control it and even turn it to our advantage.

This book has arisen out of detailed study in Manchester and includes more general observations on towns throughout England and Wales. But there is clearly a great deal in common between British urban problems and those of many other European countries. Despite the demolition and rebuilding that arose from the ravages of war, the housing problem (both in terms of numbers and standards and in terms of the ages of the buildings) has many similar features in most of these countries.[1] Although they will receive little attention in this book, it is probably true to say that much of our argument is valid for them.

Most British towns are basically radial, in that they have a centre from which roads radiate. Some have grown out of small villages and still retain signs of their old centre, often as a church in the middle of an area now so devoted to shops and commerce that the ancient parish is almost uninhabited. In the less industrialised areas it is still possible for us to find near some towns replicas of their earlier selves, in the form of villages in which one sees not just the difference of scale, but also the effects of this difference on form and function, and vice versa. In particular we can see how, as the towns

have grown outwards through the accretion of new buildings around
the fringe, the old centre has often been redeveloped, for reasons we
shall shortly examine. Sometimes a hill, a river, a railway or a
geological difficulty has distorted the radial pattern of growth.
Roads have often encouraged a ribbon development in the van of a
more general spread, leading to the formation of a star-like pattern.
More recently the advent of the motor-bus and the motor-car and
the green-belt policy have combined to build up the gaps between the
radial roads, restoring to the town a more concentrated shape.
Common observation reveals that as one moves outwards from the
central business district one passes first through an area of decay,
and then through areas that tend to improve markedly—at least so
far as the condition of the buildings is concerned—until one reaches
a village that has become suburb, or the very edge of the growing
town. In many towns one may find development suggesting a theory
of concentric zones of urban development. This was propounded in
modern times by Burgess,[2] who suggested that a central zone would
be surrounded by a transitional zone, made up of old houses, often
decaying, and being developed for business or industrial purposes.
Beyond this would be the working men's zone, and farther afield
the more costly developments of the residential zone. As a description
it was not new. Aristotle had observed the phenomenon, and Engels
had described Manchester of the 1840s in similar terms. He identified
'a fairly large commercial district' in the centre of the city, 'almost
entirely given over to offices and warehouses. Nearly the whole of
this district has no permanent residents and is deserted at night. . . .
Around this commercial quarter is a belt of built up areas . . . which
is occupied entirely by working-class dwellings. . . . Beyond this
belt . . . lie the districts inhabited by the middle classes and the
upper classes.' He went on to describe how the upper classes 'can
travel from their houses to their places of business in the centre of
the town by the shortest routes, which run entirely through working-
class districts, without even realising how close they are to the misery
and filth which lie on both sides of the road. This is because the main
streets which run from the Exchange in all directions out of the
town are occupied almost uninterruptedly on both sides by shops,
which are kept by members of the lower middle classes.'

The shops were kept 'in a clean and respectable condition', but
often they just served 'as a facade for the workers' grimy cottages'
occupying the unseen acres between the radial roads: 'it is possible

for someone to live for years in Manchester and to travel daily to and from his work without ever seeing a working-class quarter . . . mainly because the working-class districts and the middle-class districts are quite distinct'.[3]

Here is a description of a Manchester of which there is still evidence. It would, however, be wrong to suppose that a radial development must necessarily lead to a concentric development. The quality, character and extent of a given 'belt' depends very much on the direction in which one walks from the centre. For this there may be many reasons. Engels remarked that the 'eastern and north-eastern districts of Manchester are the only ones in which the middle classes have not built any houses for themselves. This is because for ten or eleven months in the year the winds blowing from the west and the south-west always carry the smoke from the factories—and there is plenty of it—over this part of the town. The workers alone can breathe this polluted atmosphere.'[4] It is in this part of Manchester, where most of the smoke is now domestic, that decay is today most prevalent.

There can, of course, be other reasons for sectoral differences. In 1939 Homer Hoyt put forward a cogent theory based on an analysis of a large number of American cities, explaining how existing sectoral characteristics tend to expand outwards along the main roads and railways that lead to the areas still undeveloped or of appropriate land value.[5] The details need not concern us. All that we need note is that in many towns where sectoral differences have existed for a long time and where areas have been developed differently and subsequently undergo changes in different ways and at different rates, we can expect the incidence of decay to be directional, as well as dependent partly on the distance from the centre. Certainly this is the case in Manchester, as our own survey has shown.

One can obtain further guidance to the origins of some of today's decay by looking not at the location of building, but at its quality and spacing. In the cotton towns of Lancashire the great growth began in the last third of the eighteenth century. It paralleled that of the cotton industry,[6] whose growth was to become one of the mightiest and most spectacular industrial phenomena of all time. Based on technical innovations that were most economic when operated on a large scale—especially after the introduction to Manchester of steam power in a cotton mill in 1789—it was a growth made possible only through the erection of a large number of houses for the workers who were so eagerly sought by the mill-owners. From agricultural areas all over the country, including the South,[7] people flocked to work in the mills, attracted by the offer of higher wages than the land afforded and by the knowledge that housing was available. Much of this housing was speculative, just as much was built by the mill-owners themselves. The accommodation within each house was often superior to that of farm cottages, but, partly to save land and partly to save materials, houses were built terraced and often back to back in narrow streets.[8] As the cotton industry grew, so did the labour force, and street after street of crowded houses began to generate many of the city's present urban problems. Had these houses been larger, or detached, or with gardens—had there, in short, been more space in and around them—many of our problems would now be easier to solve. Yet such improvements in design would have added to costs, and in one way or another these would have been passed on to the worker, and eventually would have affected the price of cotton goods. On the other hand, better housing might well have had favourable effects on production through its influence on the health of the workers. In the short-run, at least, this would probably be less important. We cannot say whether the impact on the growth of our exports would have been important, but it is likely that to some extent our rapid growth was made possible by the cheapness of our housing. To that unknown extent our present problems are part of the price we have now to pay for those of our current benefits, which derive from the rapid industrial growth with which the slums are associated.

Even at the time they were erected, these houses evoked criticism. As far back as 1782 'the Police Commissioners for Manchester took powers in their local Act to insist on party walls. This was in order to prevent spread of fire . . .'[9], but the regulations were often unobserved. In 1830 it was legislated that 'no street or court should be laid out of a less width than eight yards'.[10] Other legislation followed, and much of it was very effective. The houses built in 1850 were very different from those erected in 1820, but the former and those of the next few decades constitute our main problem. Rarely were they larger or more liberally spaced than they had to be to conform to minimum standards of the time. The need was for a great deal of cheap housing, and one way of meeting it was to cramp.

The radial development of towns, with the consequent concentration of older properties in the centre, is one of the causes of the common central-area problem. For reasons we shall consider later, there are several forces, mainly economic, that encourage central redevelopment. Decay is replaced by new buildings, but often the thriving centre is separated from spacious pleasant suburbs by a roughly concentric area of very little change. On its outer edges change is rather sluggish. A little new building occurs. A filling-station replaces a cinema. Adjacent houses are converted into a shop. Perhaps a small supermarket is established. As one moves towards the centre, the evidence of change is greater. Streets that were once residential are devoted to commercial purposes. Whatever the reason for these changes, the fact is that while the form and structure of the converted building usually show only slight change, the function has changed considerably.

Closer to the centre there will be a greater number of properties in each street where the occupiers will have made structural altera-tions, often at great expense, to adapt at least the front of the build-ing to its new function. Too often, however, adequate adaptation is too costly, and unsightly extensions, frequently made of unsuitable materials and with no regard to appearance, appear in the back-yards. These adapted commercial premises usually generate more traffic than they did as houses. Lack of adequate access from the rear often causes loading and unloading to be done across the pavement. Sometimes this results in double-parking because the road is already lined with parked cars. On the fringe of the centre, changing function and insufficient adaptation have added to congestion.

In areas such as these, little new building takes place, except through the creeping outward extension of the centre itself. Here are the slum shops, dependent mainly on the residents of the slum houses behind them. Once profiting from commuters' purchases, now they often see those decline because of parking difficulties. There is no incentive to spend more than the minimum on maintenance to permit the present functions to continue, albeit less efficiently as time goes by. Before redeveloping or selling, the landlords wait for the growing central district to expand far enough to cause local land values to rise: and they know that they may have to wait for a long time. The residents of the houses that replaced the 'workers' grimy cottages' behind Engels's 'facade' of shops sometimes try to improve the appearance of the houses they rent, but often they seem to be fighting a losing battle against litter, parked cars and the general deterioration of the surroundings. Some wish to move, while many of those nearest to the centre prefer to remain where they are, but long for amenities the rest of us take for granted.[11]

Just as the drabness of a railway station is broken by the brightness of its bookstall, so this gloomy scene is often relieved by a corner pub, where the brewers have continued to invest money in maintaining, and even improving, their property, or to a lesser extent by a modernised bank. In both cases there has been negligible change of function. The design of a public house of two or three centuries ago may be perfectly appropriate to the needs of today, while the bank built eighty years ago may still be adequate. Is there a clue here to some relationship between functional obsolescence and physical condition?

Another slightly different example comes to mind. Many churches and rectories in otherwise decrepit areas show how squalor can be eliminated on a minimum budget through attention to the fabric of the building and to cleanliness. Sometimes the function of the rectory has slightly changed because families are now smaller and domestic staff more costly, but the function of the church is older than the building itself. Its function now is the same as it was when, in the Middle Ages, the 'Church was the first to realize that city land could be made to pay' through 'parcelling out the church domains into very small plots and selling them for the erection of booths from which candles, holy pictures, and even quite mundane articles might be sold' to the pilgrims.[12] We shall refer again to the consequences of this constancy of function.

We have spoken of shops and houses, but slums are not restricted to these. The slum is the extreme state of structural or environmental decay, brought about by economic, social or other factors, where the standard of fitness for purpose has fallen below the level at which palliatives might be acceptable. By modern standards and by this definition many schools are so inadequate that they must be classed as slums.[13] So must some offices and many public lavatories. Whether it is appropriate to refer to some parks, car-parks, bus stations, cinemas and motorway service-stations in these terms is a matter we consider later. We can, however, suggest that where there is an excessive pressure of use on an inadequately designed space, an environmental deterioration of a kind that tends to lead to slums is likely to take place: but slums can also arise in other ways, and one of these is a failure to make good the natural decay to which all buildings are subject.

Some building decay is physical and, some is chemical. High winds and the eroding effect of rain can weaken and eventually destroy the most substantial buildings. Porous bricks and stones (such as Bathstone and many sandstones) can be subjected to considerable strain in cold weather through the expansion of absorbed water as it freezes. Eventually these materials show signs of 'fatigue', splitting and flaking. Timber and other materials can be similarly affected.[14]

> The great enemy of most of the sedimentary rocks is pollution of the atmosphere. Nothing has been so fatal to the preservation of English stonework as the smoky air of industrialism. Deterioration of stone has been very much more rapid in the past 150 years than at any time previously. Wood smoke did no harm at all. Now, for some sandstone and nearly all limestone buildings in towns, the sulphur-laden air means certain destruction, since even rainwater is changed into dilute sulphuric acid.[15]

This is an aspect of decay that is of increasing importance. Despite the success of smoke-control orders in reducing the amount of particulate pollution, sulphur dioxide pollution is increasing, especially in the vicinity of chemical works. Highly soluble in water, it falls as sulphurous acid, which reacts chemically with various kinds of stone and other materials. In the normal course of events the action is slow, but in heavily polluted areas it may be so fast that the building succumbs to chemical decay before natural weathering would have had serious effects upon it. The only remedies appear to be stricter control of pollution (which may be so costly as to be uneconomical, although this is a subject on which little convincing evidence exists) or the use of materials (including new materials) that are acid-resistant.

It is partly because the weather and atmospheric pollution, on the one hand, and building materials, on the other, differ from place to place that we must expect wide variations in the 'natural life' of a building. Here the words 'from place to place' have to be interpreted not only as 'between regions', but also as 'between locations'. A building may be sheltered from the weather by another building or some natural feature.

The 'natural life'[16] of a given building in a given place can usually be extended by maintenance-work, and there are few buildings to which such work is never done. There may well come a time, however, in the life of any building, where for one reason or another the owner decides that it is not profitable to spend more upon it. Perhaps it is deteriorating so rapidly that repairs are too costly. Possibly the building is no longer suitable for its original purpose, and so brings in an income not commensurate with maintenance-costs. Sometimes the reason may be that the site will soon be required for another purpose. These and other reasons will be examined later. All that we need to note now is that once this stage is reached, when expenditure on maintenance falls short of what is required, then accelerated decay is bound to begin.

The consequences of decay are as varied and complex as its causes. From an economist's viewpoint, decay represents depreciation of an asset, and there is the permanent question of whether to spend resources on maintenance, to redevelop or to leave alone. In the first two cases immediate costs are involved. In the last case there are no immediate direct costs, but there may well be indirect costs, including, for example, dangers to health, environmental decline or falling values of neighbouring property. Questions of taxation, subsidies, compulsory purchase and compensation arise.

At this stage, economic and social consequences begin to merge. We think not only of the owners of these properties, but also of the communities that live in them. Do decaying houses and bad environment go together? Are the families that live in decaying areas different from those who live elsewhere?

In our next chapter we look at the relationships between the physical decay of houses, the condition of the environment and various social characteristics. The following chapter looks more closely at the sociology of residential slums. We then consider a different kind of decaying area, illustrated by a detailed account of a small non-residential part of a twilight zone in Manchester. In these ways we learn something about the forces that cause decay in both residential and commercial areas. Chapter 5 attempts to weave these ideas into a theory, and gives an account of an urban simulation model that is being developed in the Centre for Urban and Regional Research at Manchester University. The last chapter discusses matters of policy.

CHAPTER 2

Physical Decay, the Environment and the Household

Some relationships between the physical decay of houses, the nature of the environment and various social characteristics are brought out through a survey that was done, as part of the Civic Trust inquiry, in Manchester and two of its contiguous towns—Salford and Stretford.

Essentially our procedure was to assess the physical conditions of about 2000 houses and other buildings, and also to give a mark to the environment around each of these buildings. Other information from population-census results enabled us to examine a number of possible correlations.

Our survey was done with very limited resources and was intended to be as much an exploration into method as a means of obtaining data. The three towns of Manchester, Salford and Stretford had a population in 1961 of 874,850. They form part of a larger continuous urban area. The historical boundaries between them have long ceased to divide the one from the other, even though they are governed locally by three separate councils. The broad idea was to examine a sample of buildings by looking at them from the outside, and to give them marks for their apparent condition, as indicated by such features as peeling paint, surface deterioration, displacement of roof units, broken glazing, leaking gutters or down pipes, evidence of settlement, timber rot and sagging roofs. More detail is given in Appendix 1.

The area we studied was divided into forty-one squares of two-kilometre side. In each square forty-nine points were selected at random, in a way described in the appendix. The observer reported on the condition of the building to whose curtilage the point was closest, provided that it was within thirty paces. This method was not quite the same as choosing buildings at random, since it meant that large buildings stood a larger chance of being chosen than small ones.

As a result of this survey, each building was given a decay mark. This ranged from 0 to 60, increasing with the amount of decay. Plates 1–8 illustrate the kind of condition leading to various values of this mark. The marks had a frequency distribution shown in Figure 1. It is possible that further work of this kind may enable us to make some generalisations about decay curves of this kind.

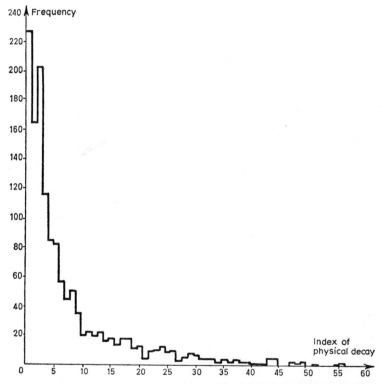

Figure 1. Frequency distribution of decay marks for buildings investigated in Manchester–Salford–Stretford survey

Another way of presenting the data is to calculate the mean decay marks, one for each square. These are shown in Figure 2. They are, of course, only estimates of the results obtainable if we had been able to inspect every single property. Their reliability

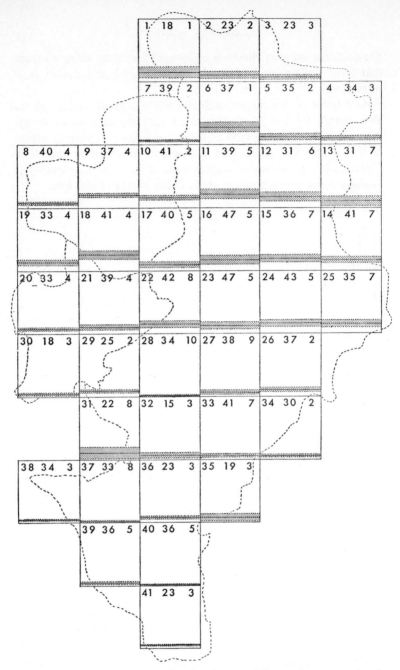

Figure 2. Mean decay marks for the two-kilometre squares in the Manchester–Salford–Stretford survey

The numbers indicate (1) the square, (2) the number of points with associated buildings, and (3) the identity of the observer

depends on the number of properties actually examined and the range of quality within the square. Even square 6, which had a decay index of 16·4, had five buildings with no apparent defects, and another five with a mark of 3 or less. It also had three properties that scored 44 marks each out of a possible 60. At the other end of the scale the square with the lowest average mark (square 37, scoring an average of 0·9) had two-thirds of its buildings in perfect condition, but also had one scoring 18 adverse marks.

It is here that our attempt to select the buildings at random comes to our aid. Actually, as we explained, we selected locations at random, but inspection of large-scale maps suggests that, except in one or two squares, where there were particularly large properties, it is not unreasonable to apply confidence tests applicable to random samples. We calculated the range on either side of the sample mean in which there was a 95 per cent probability that the true mean result (which would have been revealed if we had looked at all properties) would lie. This was done for each square. Thus in square 10 the sample mean index of decay is 10·2, while the true value for the square would probably lie between 8·0 and 12·4.

A glance at Figure 2 or at Table A1.3 (p. 122), where the detailed results are given, shows that our confidence bands are rather wide. To take an extreme example, in square 31 the true mean has a 95 per cent chance of lying between 0·6 and 12·0. The widest ranges either coincide with fairly high average means (and are explicable by the wide variation of property condition in the square as in square 16, where there is considerable redevelopment occurring) or occur in squares where, because of parks or wasteland, the number of buildings actually examined fell very considerably, as in square 1. Appendix 1 examines the consequences of taking larger samples.

The regular nature of the distribution, and the fact that even with a small sample it is possible to observe significant differences between squares, encouraged us to feel that the method was of some use. Appendix 1 describes modifications of this method, which have since been used in other inquiries. Further support for it comes from Figure 3, which shows all of the points for which we recorded decay marks. The locations were grouped into four equal sets. The buildings that had the highest mark formed one set, and these are shown by the largest circles on the map. The buildings that fell into the next highest quartile are shown by slightly smaller circles, and so on. Anybody who knows the Manchester area will immediately see the

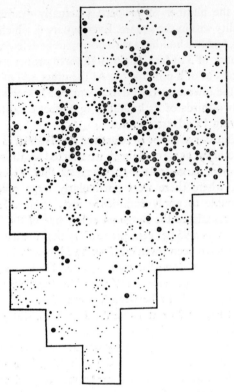

Figure 3. Location of points studied that had an associated building in the Manchester–Salford–Stretford survey. The larger the circle the worse the decay of the building

result he would expect, with most of the severely decayed buildings in the northern half of the area.

It should be possible to do a detailed study of a sample of buildings with decay marks in the range 20–29 and to use this as the basis of an estimate of the resources that would be required to bring the buildings up to a specified standard. A similar analysis for other ranges would then enable us to do a quick survey of a town along the lines indicated above, to draw the frequency distribution, and from it to estimate the resource requirements that various policies of improvement and renewal might require.

A question posed in the first chapter was that of the possible relationship between different kinds of decay. One of particular

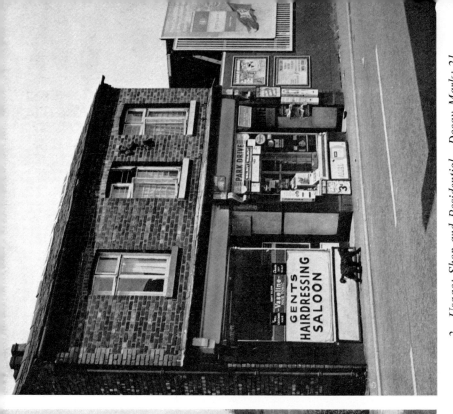

2 Usage: Shop and Residential   Decay Mark: 21

1 Usage: Residential   Decay Mark: 0

4   Usage: Residential   Decay Mark: 44

3   Usage: Residential   Decay Mark: 30

6　Usage: Shop and Residential　Decay Mark: 22

5　Usage: Residential　Decay Mark: 9

8   Usage: Residential   Decay Mark:: 43

7   Usage: Residential   Decay Mark: 29

interest is the quality of the environment. A rail journey across
Northern England, from Manchester by the Rochdale line to Leeds,
reveals a collection of shale tips, stagnant water ponds, rubbish
dumps, blackened cottages and shacks, littered streets, boarded
windows and disused mills. Here one finds the barren, forlorn decay,
so sensitively and emotionally captured by Lowry. Here is a mixture
of physical decay of buildings and a more general environmental
decay. How closely are they associated?

The survey we have just described enables us to answer this, for
we also required the observers to report on characteristics of the
environment around each point visited. It will be recalled that
several of the points had no buildings within thirty paces, but it was

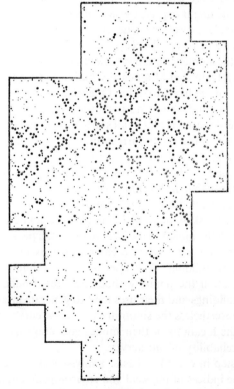

*Figure 4. Location of all points studied, with or without an associated
building, in the Manchester–Salford–Stretford survey. The larger the
circle the worse the environment*

still possible to record the presence or absence of trees, litter, air pollution, offensive smells and noise. From these data an index of environmental quality was compiled, as described in Appendix 1. For ease of comparison with our index of physical decay this is devised in such a way that the value increases as the environment becomes worse. Figure 4, which is similar to Figure 3, shows the locations of the points visited, with the largest circles representing the worst environment. A visual comparison with Figure 3 immediately shows not only the location of points for which we measured the environment, even though there was no building, but the very considerable similarity of the distributions. Bad environment and decaying buildings seem to go together.

These marks were averaged to form estimates for the forty-one squares. As one might expect, the confidence bands within which we could reasonably expect the true value to lie are much narrower than in the case of physical decay. There are three reasons for this. One is that the immediate environment of a building is less likely to differ much from that of a near-by building, even if the buildings themselves are more likely to differ. Offensive smells and air pollution tend to blow around. A second is that the highest possible score is lower. The third reason is that in all squares we looked at the environment at all forty-nine points, irrespective of whether there was an associated building.

Figures 5 and 6 show the distributions of the environmental scores for points that in the first case have and in the second case do not have associated buildings. In both cases the distribution may be described as a skew unimodal curve, but it is interesting to note that in Figure 5 the modal mark is higher (i.e. the peak is more to the right) than in Figure 6. Adverse environment is more common in the presence of buildings than elsewhere. This simply reflects such facts as that often the points without associated buildings were in parks, that buildings and their uses tend to generate litter and smells, and so on. Nevertheless the smoothness of these curves, their general shapes and the locations of their modes encourage us to have some faith in the reliability of our survey.

The next step in our Manchester analysis was to see how closely correlated the indices of physical and environmental decay might be. Once the calculations for the confidence limits have been performed, it is a short step to obtaining the correlation coefficient between the values of the two indices. These have been worked out for the

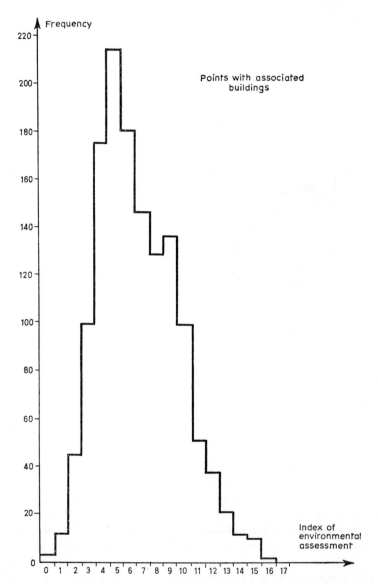

Figure 5. Frequency distribution of environmental scores for points with associated buildings in the Manchester–Salford–Stretford survey

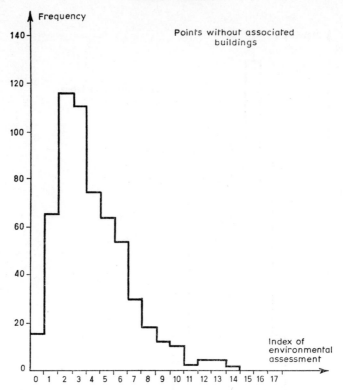

Figure 6. Frequency distribution of environmental scores for points without associated buildings in the Manchester–Salford–Stretford survey

buildings in each square and listed in Appendix 1. For samples of this size the coefficients that are numerically less than about 0·4 should be ignored, as such values could easily arise by pure chance. We can see that for the buildings in some squares there is no significant correlation between the two variables. In other squares there seems to be a strong association. Here, however, we could easily fall into a trap, for the theory behind the correlation formula requires that if the points are plotted on a scattergram, then they should lie reasonably within an ellipse. To check whether this was so we drew scattergrams for several of the squares. We show that for square 13, which had a positive correlation coefficient of 0·74. The result is best described as the right-hand half of a vertical ellipse, the straight edge

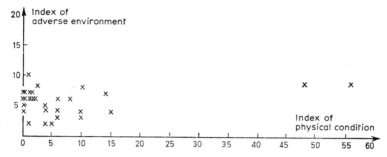

Figure 7. Scattergram for square 13 in Manchester–Salford–Stretford survey

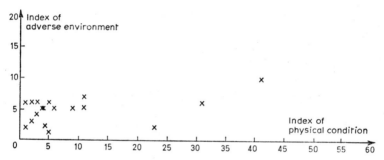

Figure 8. Scattergram for square 1 in Manchester–Salford–Stretford survey

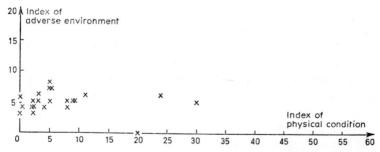

Figure 9. Scattergram for square 2 in Manchester–Salford–Stretford survey

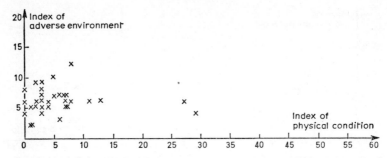

Figure 10. Scattergram for square 4 in Manchester–Salford–Stretford survey

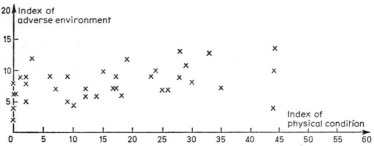

Figure 11. Scattergram for square 6 in Manchester–Salford–Stretford survey

being formed by the vertical (environment) axis, with two remote and isolated points rather high up and a long way off to the right as in Figure 7. Scattergrams for other squares were equally unsatisfactory. It is quite clear that correlation coefficients for such distributions are likely to be misleading. Actually, if the calculation is repeated with the two extreme points omitted, then by pure chance we obtain a correlation coefficient of exactly the same size, but negative. Not even this means much for such a semi-elliptical distribution. Figures 8–11 show the distribution for some other squares. These results are not really surprising. In the middle of a bad environment there may easily be a building, or a whole street of buildings, in good condition. It may be one that has been well looked after, or it could have been built only a year earlier. What all of this does show is that the person who looks superficially at an area and describes it as a slum, judging it by factors such as those listed in our environment index, may quite overlook the condition of the buildings; and if the main fault in these is external grime, he may go away advocating a policy for slum-clearance that would entail the demolition of a high percentage of sound buildings. It may, of course, be good social or planning policy to demolish such buildings in the light of other or wider considerations.

While the results of an investigation into whether the index of decay for a given building is closely associated with the index of environment have been negative, there may still be something of an association when we look at wider areas. To test this we have drawn

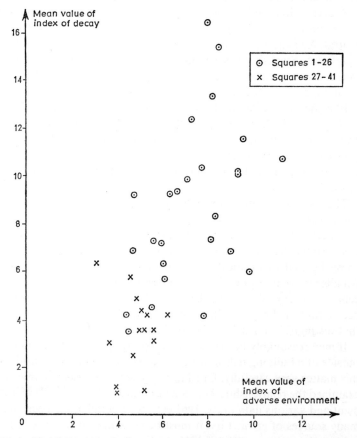

Figure 12. Scattergram for mean value of index of adverse environment and mean value of index of decay for each of the forty-one squares in the Manchester–Salford–Stretford survey

in Figure 12 a scattergram showing the means for the forty-one squares. Measuring the mean index of decay horizontally and the index of environment vertically, we plotted forty-one points and numbered each one with its square number. At first sight there seems to be a fairly close fit within an ellipse, but there is a clustering in the lower left-hand quarter. There seem to be two overlapping ellipses. One has its points fairly scattered, and contains all the points for the squares numbers 1 to 26. The other, which has its points more closely clustered, is for squares 27–41, with the exclusion of square 31, which is shown by the highest cross in Figure 12.

A correlation analysis of the mean values of the decay index and the environment index for the twenty-six squares in northern and central Manchester yields a coefficient of 0·54, which is highly significant. Statistically speaking, about a quarter of the variation in the decay index can be 'explained' by variation in the environmental index, or vice versa.

For the remaining fourteen squares, excluding square 31, the coefficient is 0·22, which is not significant. Thus, whereas in north and central Manchester a square that is environmentally bad (or good) tends to have much (or little) decay, there is no such tendency in southern Manchester. It is a result that emphasises the importance of local studies.

There is a temptation for us to take our reasoning a step further, and to conclude from these results that there is no significant correlation between decay and environment until a certain level of decay has been reached, when a positive association sets in, as though any decay beyond this critical level generates an adverse environment. An alternative interpretation is that excessively adverse environment generates decay. We cannot here assert that these suggestions have been established beyond all doubt, because of the many other factors that distinguish north Manchester from the south.

It may reasonably be argued that a purely visual inspection of the outside of a building tells us little about its condition. We considered this matter very carefully. One fairly objective test was possible. We examined the relationships between our indices of decay and environment and various data in the 1961 census of population. There were many sources of error. First it must be remembered that the census information relates to April 1961, and that by January 1965, when the field survey was carried out, much would have changed. Not only would decay have advanced in many areas, but often large areas of building had disappeared altogether. One cannot be certain that the results would have been better had the two sets of data related to the same point in time, but it does seem to be likely.

Another source of error is that the field survey related to *all buildings*, while the census was concerned with dwellings only. It would be possible to extract from the field-survey data the information relating to residential buildings only and then to compare that by correlation methods with the census data. This was indeed considered, but in the event the data-retrieval problem would have held up these first results.

The most obvious source of trouble arises from our choice of squares. We had forty-one, containing an average of over 7000 dwellings, and from each we sampled a maximum of forty-nine buildings. These grid squares occupy the same territory as over 1200 enumeration districts. Many finer-grained relationships are therefore lost. Not the least reason for the choice of a two-kilometre square as a basis for the collection and processing of data was the pressure of time and the need to economise on occasional staff. There is little doubt that the use of one-kilometre or half-mile squares would have greatly reduced the amount of variation encountered within each square and revealed the 'grain' of the critical relationship more clearly. As it was, however, when we designed the survey, the idea of comparison with the census data had not occurred to us, and so we had to try to identify the squares with sets of enumeration districts. The number of districts lying partly in one square and partly in another was small compared with the total. To avoid arbitrary splitting of enumeration-district data between squares, we decided to adopt a 'best fit' approximation. For each square we aggregated the data for that set of whole enumeration districts most closely approximating to the squares.

There were forty-one squares in all, but squares 37–41 cover a large segment of Wythenshawe, where the peculiar characteristics of extensive post-war housing development—added to those of the pre-war garden suburb, with very low rates of owner-occupation, young tenants, and so on—tend to upset the pattern that has developed over the rest of Manchester. For this reason we calculated our correlation coefficients first for the forty-one squares and then for the smaller population of thirty-six squares.

When Wythenshawe is excluded, our index of decay has several very significant associations with the census data. The strongest is with the exclusive use of domestic facilities. The houses that were most decayed (judged from the outside) were those in which the non-sharing households were least likely to have exclusive use of all basic amenities. The correlation coefficient of -0.7075 is very significant, and indicates that about half of the variance in our index can be 'explained' by variance in the amenities. The inclusion of Wythenshawe, with its new modern houses and the quality houses of its inter-war development, makes the conclusion even stronger.

Rather interestingly, the next highest correlation coefficient, which is also negative, is that between decay and the radial distance from central Manchester (measured from the centre of the relevant square to the mid-point of the boundary between squares 16 and 17, this being roughly the junction of Mosley Street and Princess Street). Here the coefficient of -0.5185 is again highly significant for the thirty-six squares. Decay decreases as we move outwards from the centre, and about a quarter of its variance can be 'explained' by the distance. When we allow Wythenshawe to influence the result, the co-efficient improves to -0.6220, 'explaining' over a third of the variance.

Four more census measures are well correlated with decay in thirty-six squares. As the proportion of owner-occupiers rises, the severity of decay declines. Houses with many persons per room are likely to be in bad condition, as are dwellings in the squares containing most houses or most people. In all of these cases there are very significant correlations. The results relating to the density of development are not substantially altered by the inclusion of Wythenshawe, but for the other variables there is no longer any significant correlation. We found that neither with nor without Wythenshawe did the proportion of households who were sharing accommodation, or the percentage of households of two persons containing at least one pensioner, have any significant association with decay.

The results, even when qualified by the many imperfections in our statistics, are sufficiently interesting and, on reflection, sensible to encourage us to feel that with greater resources our method of external assessment may lead to reasonably valid and useful conclusions. Neither our index nor the census of population results can be a complete measure of the state of the building. Our index is concerned with a visual inspection of the outside. The census data concerns amenities that are largely internal fittings. It tells us whether there is a bath, but not whether the bath or the bathroom is fit to be used. Yet, as we have seen, the outside appearance and the

TABLE 1. CORRELATION BETWEEN MEASURES OF DECAY AND SELECTED CENSUS VARIABLES IN MANCHESTER–SALFORD–STRETFORD SURVEY

(A) Using squares 1–36 inclusive ONLY

	Arithmetic mean	Standard deviation	Correlation coeffic. with building decay	Correlation coeffic. with environmental decay
Number of dwellings	7514·36	3802·28	0·4389	0·3663
Overall population density (persons/acre)	22·72	12·04	0·4233	0·3595
Average persons per room	0·65	0·07	0·5116	0·5703
Percentage of households sharing accommodation	4·31	5·15	−0·2049	−0·0891
Percentage of households, owner-occupiers	37·82	15·73	−0·5149	−0·6971
Percentage of non-sharing households: exclusive use amenities	70·91	20·16	−0·7075	−0·8117
Percentage households with at least one pensioner	21·42	2·33	0·0815	0·0296
Distance from central Manchester (in km)	4·66	1·78	−0·5185	−0·7213
Average score for buildings, building decay	7·40	3·60		
Average score for grid square, environment decay	307·64	99·16		

(B) Using squares 1–41, i.e. all squares

	Arithmetic mean	Standard deviation	Correlation coeffic. with building decay	Correlation coeffic. with environmental decay
Number of dwellings	7283·22	3634·83	0·4507	0·3964
Overall population density (person/acre)	22·38	11·41	0·3998	0·3564
Average persons per room	0·66	0·08	0·1621	0·2176
Percentage of households sharing accommodation	3·85	4·98	−0·0647	0·0232
Percentage of households, owner-occupiers	34·17	17·71	−0·1309	−0·3046
Percentage of non-sharing households; exclusive use amenities	74·15	20·80	−0·7595	−0·8421
Percentage of households with at least one pensioner	20·64	3·46	0·2794	0·2580
Distance from central Manchester (in km)	5·32	2·47	−0·6220	−0·7317
Average score for buildings, building decay	6·76	3·80		
Average score for grid square, environment decay	292·20	102·01		

internal fittings are well correlated. The suggestion that decay may be more associated with the density of occupation in terms of persons per room than with the number of households involved is a very reasonable one, as are the other results just described. A point in favour of our index, when compared with the census data, is that sagging roofs, broken glass and surface deterioration will all exist long after every household has exclusive use of all amenities. When our present areas of greatest decay have been renewed and our inter-war houses begin to decay, the more fundamental nature of this kind of index will be all too apparent.

The index of environmental quality was associated with fewer census statistics than was the index of physical decay. On the other hand, its correlations with the exclusive use of domestic facilities and with the distance from central Manchester remained the strongest, and were even more marked than for the index of decay. Areas with a high proportion of owner-occupiers were more likely to have pleasant environments, as were areas with few persons per room, or few houses per acre. The results are given in Table 1. The close relationships between our two indices and the exclusive use of domestic facilities may, of course, be simply a reflection of age, in the same way as the distance outwards from Manchester's centre tends to reflect the date of buildings.*

These rather tentative observations about physical decay, environment, overcrowding, owner-occupation and other factors lead us to more fundamental sociological questions. The next chapter is written by Miss Gittus, who has made a special study of some of them.

* This examination of the relationships between the indices and the Census data was undertaken by Mr McLoughlin.

CHAPTER 3

Sociological Aspects of Urban Decay

by Elizabeth Gittus

Social studies of the urban slum developed historically, in this country at least, out of concern for the 'slum-dweller'. The slum was usually defined in terms of a scarcity of such basic amenities as living-space, open space, drainage and sanitation, which was in violation of standards of public health and likely to be conducive to squalor and disease.

More recently, with progress in the clearance or refurbishing of slum areas, interest in their population has been focused on the incidence among them of a wider range of social problems—crime, immorality, mental illness, poverty—in family breakdown, and, in some studies, in the emergence of a way of life that was labelled, not always with adequate evidence or conceptualisation, as the 'sub-culture' of the slum or a state of social disorganisation.

The social-disorganisation approach has been criticised as tending to confusion and circularity of argument, for it is difficult to appreciate or define the concept without reference to forms of behaviour such as crime, suicide, child-neglect, mental defectiveness, which are usually observed and reported as consequences of it.[1]

In this analysis of the sociological aspects of living in the midst of decay, the concept of decay will be reserved for the structure of buildings and the general appearance of the locality. Decay, even in these terms, is manifest in more ways than one. It is evident, in this country, in the existence of two fairly distinctive types of decaying area.

One is characterised by the inadequacy and obsolescence of the buildings themselves, whether the dreary terraces of cottage-like dwellings that were slung out across the mid- or late-nineteenth-century city at the first rush of urbanisation, or the grim Victorian tenements with courts and balconies still awaiting demolition in parts of East London, Liverpool, Glasgow and in other cities of their vintage.

In the second type of area the onset of decay has been preceded or accompanied by a change in the occupancy of the buildings and in the essential character of their use. A fine Victorian town-house falls vacant on the owner's death. It is bought up, subdivided and its rooms let, often with the minimum of provision for the maximum rent, to tenants who are only too glad to find accommodation. This happens again and again, and soon the character of the area is changed and its function shifted from that of town residence for the wealthy to that of a place of refuge for a transient population, often varied in nationality and in class. This is already a familiar pattern in the Abercromby district of Liverpool, in the Rye-Hill area of Newcastle upon Tyne and in Manchester's Moss Side.

The first type of decaying area has been called a 'residual' area. Eventually it will disappear, one hopes, from the urban scene. The second type has been aptly described as 'transitional'. Its character is changing, but its location may also shift to wherever the type of large house with facilities for adaptation and sub-letting is available to meet the needs of the city's immigrant or foot-loose minority or to satisfy the avarice of the exploiters of the housing market.[2]

While the distinction between these two types of area is not always so clear-cut, it is one to recognise. In economic terms it approximates to the distinction between physical and economic blight. Sociologically it is important to distinguish between the residual slum area where people live or have lived in family groups over a long period of time and the transitional rooming-house district. A recent review of urban sociology from the Chicago school has criticised some studies for having failed to make this contrast.[3] In a recent analysis of slums and community development in India, Marshall Clinard notes three types of slum area: the tenement, comparable to the residual area of the western city, the run-down neighbourhood, the counterpart of the transitional zone, and the shanty town or squatter colony.[4]

The following questions, relating to the populations of decaying neighbourhoods, will now be considered, using the residual/transitional dichotomy:

1. Are there demographic and other sociological differences between the populations of such areas and those of other city localities?

2. Are social problems more prevalent here than elsewhere?

3. If so, have the inhabitants, by their way of life and/or predisposing tendencies contributed to the onset of the areas' decay, or are the roots of such anti-social behaviour to be found within the areas themselves?

It must be understood that the discovery of differences in the characteristics of the populations of these areas as compared with others does not imply a direct relationship, within the experience of the individual, between the possession of these characteristics and contact with urban decay, in either sense. Patterns of association in this field are usually ecological rather than personal, and only rarely may the latter kind of result be inferred from the former.

1

Systematic comparative studies of urban areas in this country have been few, and have been impeded until recently by the lack of data for sufficiently small areas.

Following the 1951 census, some aspects of the social structure of the conurbations of Merseyside and south-east Lancashire were compared, using the subdivisions of the conurbations that were a new feature of the census programme.[5] These subdivisions included, within each conurbation, units that approximated to the residual and transitional areas defined above. Differences in indices of population density and housing conditions were consistent with the criteria by which these areas were defined. Demographic differences were found to be consonant with theories developed in U.S.A. and elsewhere. In the residual area, within both Merseyside and south-east Lancashire, the populations were found to be above the respective conurbation average in the percentage of young children and of families at an early stage of development. Their fertility rates were high, but the sex ratio (females per 1000 males) was relatively low. These characteristics are typical of poorer working-class communities. High fertility rates have been found to be associated with low income.[6] This is not a direct relationship, and, certainly on Merseyside, other factors of parentage and religious affiliation, though not studied here, may generally be said to have contributed to the prevalence of the large family in this kind of locality.

There was also evidence for both conurbations, but especially for Merseyside, of a high percentage of families with heads who were widowed, divorced or single. This is perfectly compatible with the particular kinship-structure of this kind of area, as will be seen. In terms of social class the residual areas were found to be mainly homogeneous, with a majority of men in the lower occupational grades.

By contrast, in each conurbation the population of the transitional zone or the closest approximation to it was characterised by low fertility, high sex-ratio (both compatible with theories about the populations of such areas), a high percentage both of single persons in the adult population and of heads of households who were not married. Of this last group, many of the heads within this part of Merseyside were aged under forty. They represented, therefore, younger people living on their own, rather than, as for the residual area, groups of elderly widows living with, but separate (in housekeeping terms), from their married children. The transitional areas were distinctive too for the foreign-born elements in their population, a result that is in line with findings for Chicago and other metropolitan areas of the United States, and more recently for Paris by Chombart de Lauwe, who noted the high percentage of African residents in the *zone d'acculturation* bordering the central area.[7]

These transitional areas were more varied in social class than the residual neighbourhoods. This was a genuine variety and not, as suggested for Bethnal Green, the result of exaggerating the status of some shopkeepers and employers. In these transitional areas there is often a nucleus of professional people. It is not inconceivable that such areas may eventually be so refurbished that the professional element will increase. One research project at least is currently investigating the feasibility of such a change.[8]

These are some of the population traits that distinguish these types of areas from each other and from other urban localities. In terms of single variables, the patterns revealed here are consonant with theories about the differentiation of urban populations and with the findings of more detailed, local studies. Collectively they point to a deeper and more significant variation in the functioning within these areas of one basic social institution, i.e. the family.

The importance of the family and the cohesive nature of an extensive kinship-network within a fairly narrow locality has often been described as one of the main features of the residual type of inner urban society. The term matrilocal is unattractive, perhaps, but apposite. For the mother, even the grandmother, is the dominant figure. Poorer working-class conditions are said to favour the dominance of the female. The bond that persists between married daughter and mother, though not infrequently economic rather than social in its origin, is well established and supported by a wealth of research material and comment.[9]

The extended family is the pivot of social life, giving help in time of illness or other emergency and protection against change. For many people the life of the street is the only one that they know. They are living testimonies of the persistence of the past when conditions are favourable to its retention. Many writers have applauded the solidarity of family life in areas like these and have been apprehensive of the social disruption that might accompany rehousing, but recently the protective role of the family has come to be regarded, with some concern, as inhibiting social mobility. Those who remain within the family network are often unwilling to accept change, while young parents who are anxious to secure better prospects for themselves or their children are little deterred in their desire to move by the prospect of leaving their immediate relatives and friends.[10] Recent studies have concluded that, in any event, with modern transport facilities the extended family does continue to function, even though its members may be scattered, and that a strong sense of belonging often does persist among them.

Rosser and Harris, from a survey in Swansea designed as a comparison with the Bethnal Green studies, do not recommend that planners should concentrate on preserving the traditional community as found in these areas, and while they acknowledge that a sympathetic and informed social policy can assist the extended family to adapt to new circumstances consequent upon rehousing, they emphasise that modifications in its structure and function have come to stay.[11]

In the transitional area, by contrast, the predominant characteristic is one of variety and the absence of close family ties. This isolation, regarded in general theory as one of the adverse factors of urbanisation, is recognised as no longer applicable to all urban neighbourhoods, but has often been observed in this country and elsewhere within this transitional zone. For some people this isolation, even if accepted as inevitable, spells loneliness and misery. For others the anonymity of life in this kind of area is regarded as an asset and is deliberately sought.

Redevelopers of such areas, while usually anxious to kindle some community life and spirit among the former class of residents, must not be insensitive to those who prefer to keep their own privacy and independence.

2

Surveys of the incidence of a number of social problems within towns have consistently demonstrated their concentration in the transitional zone.[12] With the exception of juvenile crime (more common among the younger populations of the residual areas), a number of indices relating to health disorders—especially those associated with poor environmental or living conditions, aspects of child-neglect, illegitimacy, mental defect and illness—have been found to occur most frequently among the appropriate 'population at risk' in each case, in the downtown districts of the transitional areas, such as part of the Abercromby ward in Liverpool (which ranked highest among all the wards for all but one of the problems studied) and in the Rye-Hill area of Newcastle upon Tyne. For Liverpool, it is interesting to note that the survey of Merseyside conducted nearly thirty years ago, though based on registration districts, not wards, and covering a different set of problems, 'crime', 'immorality' and 'alcoholism' still showed a similar concentration.[13]

The more recent study included an assessment of the distribution of 'problem families', defined to be those with member(s) exhibiting one or more of the 'symptoms' covered. Again it showed the relative concentration of such families in the transitional ward. Similarly in Newcastle the study of variations in 'social malaise' within small areal units throughout the city has shown a relationship between this kind of composite-problem index and a score based on environmental standards. Both studies illustrate the strain that such areas impose on the various agencies for social work.

While it is tempting to relate these findings to the absence of family ties in the transitional area compared with the more stable and respectable residual area, the results, as we said earlier, are ecological not personal, and cannot, for example, be interpreted to imply a direct relationship on an individual basis, either between mental subnormality and isolation, or, conversely, between mental stability and frequent contact with family and friends. All that may be said, without evidence from a household or individual survey, is that residence in an area typified by isolation and transience increases the individual's probability of exhibiting some form of 'problem' behaviour or social ill—at least within the context of studies so far. But no explanation is implied in a statement of this kind. There have been theories, and these will now be reviewed.

3

One of the studies mentioned already made the point that areas of physical blight, in terms of the structural decay of their buildings, and those areas notorious for a high degree of social blight or social malaise were by no means coincident.[14] In other words, while the residual areas were comparatively respectable, the transitional areas contained the deviants. In considering the theories that have been advanced in explanation of this situation and of other aspects of the distribution of social problems, it must be realised that even in the worst areas these problems, whether they relate to behaviour or condition, apply to the minority of the population. It is the relative few who show signs of 'social disorganisation'. The problem families identified in the Liverpool study were fewer than the submerged tenth of all families, even in Abercromby.[15] While admittedly such individuals and families do place an exorbitant burden on the resources of the various social welfare departments and agencies, a right sense of proportion is needed in postulating any connection between pathological behaviour and adverse living conditions. Direct observations of the appalling conditions that are the lot of some of the inhabitants of these areas, far from enhancing the credibility of such an hypothesis, lead one rather to question how, if the hypothesis is valid, so many people in these circumstances manage to remain respectable and even resilient.

The problem of the transitional area becomes more urgent if considered in terms of the function that such an area represents in the life of the city. Its most disquieting aspect, and one that seems likely to continue so long as housing shortage remains, is in providing a refuge, at least temporarily, for those who do not qualify for accommodation elsewhere. A recent study of a twilight zone in Birmingham has graphically demonstrated some of the implications of this situation.[16]

The notion of the 'drift' to this type of area of those with problems already has been extended to include the possibility that people with anti-social tendencies or psychological abnormalities migrate to these areas because here they may be concealed or tolerated. One American writer has described the transitional area as a hiding-place for many services that are forbidden by the mores of the community as a whole, but which cater for the wishes of residents scattered through it.[17]

The 'drift' hypothesis focuses on the importance of predisposing psychological tendencies within the individual. Others have ascribed the existence of such 'problem areas' to the operation of precipitating, ecological factors, which derive from living in such a locality and from exposure to its culture. Some have emphasised the strains imposed by the anonymity of life there and the degree of residential mobility that it entails, while others have maintained that anonymity may be preferred, and that it is not just change but unexpected change that disturbs and disrupts.[18] While Shaw and McKay, for example, produce convincing evidence in support of the ecological explanation that views delinquency, for example, as a product of the social situation, one must admit, from the kind of functional analysis mentioned above, that in this country at least the drift hypothesis has some credibility also.[19] Louis Wirth to some extent bridges the gap by suggesting that physical aspects are conditioning factors, offering possibilities and setting limits for social and psychological existence and development.[20]

Finally, it is apparent in our present society that life in a decaying area, especially a residual one, and for all but the affluent and progressive in a transitional area, may be limited in the range of experiences and opportunities in which the individual may reasonably hope to share. Applications of decision theory to the study of social groups or strata have imputed the short-run hedonistic pattern of decision-making, in which explicit future expectations play a negligible role to the lower working classes in general and the poorer urban classes in particular.[21]

There is a style of life, a narrowness of horizon, that is consciously or unconsciously experienced by many in areas such as these. The matrilocal structure, typical of the residual areas, has been seen as tending to reinforce this situation by inhibiting desires to break away. In the transitional areas the lot of the needy minority is all the more depressing by contrast with that of their aspirant neighbours.

This state of affairs, more subtle and elusive of definition than the incidence of individual social phenomena, is regarded by some as one of the most disquieting aspects of life in these areas, being in violation of the principles currently accepted in our society, of social mobility and equality of opportunity.

Postscript

Since the manuscript for this chapter was completed, some important concepts, relevant to this discussion, have been introduced to urban research. The notion of 'housing classes', formulated by Rex and Moore[16] has been of continued interest (see J. Rex, 'The Sociology of a Zone of Transition', in R. E. Pahl (ed.) *Readings in Urban Sociology*, Pergamon Press, 1968). It represents, in a more dynamic way, the position of residents in these areas in the competition for housing facilities and the choices, if any, that are open and known to them. More recently, Ray Pahl (*Spatial Structure and Social Structure*, Centre for Environmental Studies, Working Paper No. 10) has suggested recasting the analytical framework of urban sociology in terms of the competition for land, housing, local amenities, education and other services. Others have emphasised one aspect of this competition in the involvement of local residents in the planning process (see N. Dennis, *People and Planning*, Faber & Faber (forthcoming) and J. Davies, *The Evangelical Bureaucrat*—a study of a planning exercise in Rye-Hill, Newcastle upon Tyne (awaiting publication)). New research along these lines should throw further light on some of the issues discussed here.

CHAPTER 4

Decay in a Twilight Area

The most common building in Britain is the house, and any work on urban decay must concentrate largely on the decay of houses. But in many places, and especially in and around our town centres, there is another type of decay, involving shops, offices and other business and commercial properties. Often the area of decay is a 'twilight zone' lying between a redeveloped or modernised central business area and a belt of housing constructed in the later part of the nineteenth century or in the first decade of the twentieth.

In order to appreciate the nature of urban decay we may usefully look at a detailed study of such a twilight zone, for here, unhampered by rent controls, security of tenure and other impediments, the free-market forces of demand and supply react to the functional and environmental changes that characterise a growing town. By studying them we may learn about forces operating over a wider field, even though they may be obscured by custom and legislation.

As part of the study sponsored by the Civic Trust for the North-West we looked at the Lower Deansgate area of Manchester. This is quite small, covering only about half a square mile, and a substantial part is covered by railway lines and sidings. In 1962 it had 433 separate occupiers of its premises. Some employed nobody. Others employed several hundred people. About half of the premises were offices, about a quarter shops and the remainder were chiefly warehouses or industrial.

This small non-residential area was chosen because it was on the fringe of the twilight zone. Deansgate, Manchester, contains large stores and other shops. At one end and in the centre, many of these are of high quality, but towards the other end the average quality falls. The hinterland is occupied by the mixed uses we have described. The nearest edge of the area is about ten minutes' walk from the centre of Manchester's business district.

In making our detailed study we had little to guide us. We felt that a full study of a single area could tell us a great deal about it, but we knew that our findings possibly would be of limited applicability. A sample inquiry over a wider area might have told us more, but quite apart from our inadequate knowledge of the criteria by which we could best stratify our sample, we had little idea about what we would find. Accordingly we decided to make a modest study of a small area in the hope that it would throw up ideas that might be useful in later work. Here we have not been disappointed. Our tentative conclusions may readily form hypotheses for rigorous testing. Our experience in the survey has taught us lessons, while the whole exercise has added to a general understanding of the forces of urban change.

A more detailed description of this area is given in Table 2, which also shows the number of people employed by the different land-users. It emphasises the fact that nearly three-quarters of the premises employed fewer than ten persons. On the other hand, there were also some very large employers. One railway site employed over six hundred people, and a government office had over two hundred workers in it. Four other employers had staffs of at least one hundred. The impression created by this table that shops are more likely than other land-users to have fewer than ten employees is confirmed by a chi-squared analysis.

TABLE 2. LAND-USE AND EMPLOYMENT IN LOWER DEANSGATE SURVEY

	Public Buildings	Offices	Shops	Warehouses	Industry	TOTAL
1–9 persons	8	132	95	28	46	309
10–49 persons	9	56	18	10	15	108
50 + persons	1	9	0	2	4	16
TOTAL	18	197	113	40	65	433

Other tabular analyses of the data appear in Appendix 2. These show that about half the shops were occupied by people or firms who had not moved from anywhere else, but had actually set up in the area as new concerns. This is quite different from the occupiers of offices, of whom half had moved from central Manchester. Office-occupiers tended to have premises in good condition, and a high proportion of them had been in the area for just a few years. Shops, on the other hand, were more likely than offices to be in fair or poor condition, and their occupiers were more likely to have been there longer. Industry tended to occupy premises in bad condition, and generally the smaller firms tended to be in the less good buildings.

All of these conclusions are statistically significant. They are based on chi-squared analyses and an analysis of variance. The difficulty in their interpretation arises from significant high-order interactions, which a knowledge of the area easily explains. A typical twilight area, with rather seedy offices and a high proportion of small, and sometimes unusual, shops, spattered with warehouses and industry, suddenly began to change. Before our study was contemplated there were two important forces at work. It was known that at some time an inner-ring road would pass through the area. There was also—not very far away—central-area redevelopment that was temporarily displacing a large number of tenants, and especially office tenants. Both of these forces tended to make this almost central twilight zone more attractive as a location for offices. The result was an influx within a short period of office tenants from central Manchester. This accounts for the significant interaction between land-use, duration of tenure and former location. Since these tenants tended either to go to the better buildings or to spend on improvements, interactions involving condition of building also become significant. The shopkeepers had gone to Lower Deansgate because of the low rents, almost central situation and shopping peculiarities of the area as it stood. They were not concerned with improving their new premises. Office tenants, on the other hand, had been forced to move elsewhere, and had chosen our area as a conveniently situated zone, which was acceptable if given some face-lift.

Taken by themselves these descriptive statistics of the 1962 occupiers do not tell us why there were so many recently arrived office tenants, or why shopkeepers were more likely to have originated in the area, but they do provide statistical confirmation for the less exact observations made by the alert observer. They have revealed nothing new, but they have added weight to existing impressions, including those about the impact of central redevelopment on renovation in twilight zones.

Some of these impressions were confirmed by interviews with occupiers, who also told of other reasons for the state of the area. Three case studies by Mr Eveson illustrate their stories. They were written in 1965.

Firm A occupying a site in Deansgate

This is a business that can show great expansion, and the manager wishes to expand sales and to improve his shop premises. He appreciates that this location is a little outside the recognised shopping area, but he is sure that with advertising his business could become established in the mind of the public.

However, as is the case with many occupiers in such areas, uncertainty of the future because of redevelopment plans makes any planning for the future impossible.

The land and buildings are owned by British Railways, and he has a six-monthly lease from them. He has tried to get an indication as to how long he is likely to be able to remain in these premises, but they are unable to give him any idea.

In the meantime he is looking for other premises, or for land on which to build new premises, and has apparently had no success in finding either.

He feels that he cannot go any farther out because of the lack of passing trade, and because the service he gives by delivery of goods to users who are chiefly located in the centre of the town would become less efficient.

He accepts that redevelopment of areas must take place, but objects to the lack of assistance to find new premises for the people who are to be moved.

Firm B operating a café

In the opinion of the manager, the introduction of parking meters in the town, but not in his own part of it, has led to more parking near his café. His trade has risen, and he has a better class of customer because such people as salesmen and representatives park their cars, call in for coffee and then walk to their offices nearer to the centre. Because of this change in his trade he finds that the accommodation is now too small.

He then went on to describe, from the café owner's point of view, the different locational qualities of the Piccadilly area and this area in Deansgate. In the more central café the main difficulty is getting people into the café to stay and sit down to lunch (i.e. instead of taking out lunchtime snacks and soup). His main difficulty now is that people stay in his café for a longer time, which is mainly why he considers the café accommodation to be too small.

He mentioned the difficulty of getting female labour for cafés in that area, and anywhere with a similar location slighty remote from the main shopping areas. This is because women like to wander around the shops at lunchtime, and the popular shops are too distant. This he stressed again and again. He feels that any business relying on female labour would find it very difficult to function in such areas, and virtually impossible very much farther out.

To him the obvious thing to do in redevelopment schemes is to bring the shops out to such areas as these.

Another disadvantage of this area is the fact that the premises are always being broken into (about once every three months), presumably because at night-time this area is very quiet, especially since it is non-residential.

He feels that location on the other side of Deansgate would have been better, because this would mean more passing trade from the people going to and from Knott Mill Station (which is a busy station on a fast commuter line).

This property happens to be one of those recently acquired by a property development company. As he has a lease that runs out in 1968, he feels he has a good bargaining position with this company. He stated that at the moment he is attempting to take advantage of this position so that the company either makes it worth his while to get out and/or gives a guarantee of good accommodation in the new premises to be built.

Firm C are motor factors

This firm's former premises in the area were acquired by a development company and they had to move. But the trade is strongly identified with that area, so they had to obtain premises not far away. They had no help from the corporation in their search for these, and consequently thought so ill of planners that they had not bothered to complete the Civic Trust questionnaire. In the end they could not even get planning permission to build the premises they now occupy. Desperately they bought land with planning permission for a small printing works, began to build, and 'forced the corporation to play ball with us'. They complain about the lack of any definite arrangement for the new roads in the town because this makes planning for the future of their business very difficult for them. This is because their present premises are very close to one of the proposed roads on the development plan.

These three case studies illustrate several important points—especially the impact of 'planning blight' due to uncertainty about the future, the effect of parking restrictions and the importance of neighbouring land-uses. We shall consider these later. Meanwhile it will be useful to look at the results of a second survey carried out in the same area two years later, in 1964. In this we identified firms who had moved, and then we tried to find out the reasons.

The total number of firms moving into the area (or setting up within it) during 1962–4 and still there at the time of the 1964 survey was eighty-six. Probably others had also occupied premises there between our two surveys, but had stayed for only a short while. We also recorded twelve moves within the area, while a hundred occupiers had left the area, and possibly ceased to exist.

Of the eighty-six firms known to have set up during the inter-survey period, thirteen left before a questionnaire reached them, two closed down, and one turned out to be occupying the room that its differently named parent-company had had for forty years. Thirty-eight of the remaining seventy firms were either completely new, and occupying their first premises, or they were branches of larger firms. The remaining thirty-two occupiers had previously been in accommodation outside our area.

The thirty-eight new firms or new branches set up in our area had the land-uses and size-distributions recorded in Table 3.

TABLE 3. LAND-USE AND SIZE OF 38 NEW FIRMS OR NEW BRANCHES
IN LOWER DEANSGATE SURVEY

Land-use		Size by numbers of employees	
Shopping	9	0–4 persons	26
Office	28	5–9 persons	6
Car Park	1	10–19 persons	2
		20–49 persons	1
		50 + persons	—
		unclassified	3

We have remarked that thirty-two firms moved into our area from elsewhere. In addition there were two such firms who closed down while our survey was being conducted. Table 4 is for all thirty-four firms, while the bracketed figures indicate the story for the thirty-two who remained.

In both of these tables the preponderance of offices, with shopping as second best, is clearly visible. The proportion of immigrant firms employing fewer than five persons was lower than in the case of new firms, as was the average size.

TABLE 4. LAND-USE AND SIZE OF 34 (32) IMMIGRANT FIRMS IN LOWER DEANSGATE SURVEY

Land-use			Size by number of employees		
Shopping	7	(7)	0–4 persons	13	(13)
Office	23	(23)	5–9 persons	4	(4)
Industry	1	(1)	10–19 persons	5	(5)
Warehouse	2	(1)	20–49 persons	2	(2)
Public assembly	1	(—)	50 + persons	2	(2)
			unclassified	8	(6)

Seven of the immigrants were shopkeepers—one selling food and the rest selling various kinds of consumer durables of a kind not usually found in the house—winemaking equipment, alarm systems, plastic letters, trailer equipment and so forth. Except for one of the consumer-durable shops, they all employed fewer than five persons, and while one of them had moved from premises occupied since before the war, two of them had come from shops they had entered as recently as 1961.

The food shop had moved from central Manchester (where it had rented premises since before the war) because rents and rates had risen excessively and traffic congestion and parking problems had made it difficult for callers and for the unloading of goods. The other shops moved because falling profits failed to justify the previous rent, inadequate room for expansion, termination of lease, clearance action and because departure of the parent-company to Oldham had left the subsidiary company with twice as much room as it needed. Where subsidiary reasons were mentioned, they involved the unadaptability of the previous building and traffic problems.

Most of the immigrants came to offices. There were twenty-three of them, of whom twelve came from central Manchester. Of these, five had moved because their previous premises were cleared, another five had moved because their business had expanded and there was no room to develop at their old premises. One had found that the previous premises, which they had entered ten years previously, were too large, and one seems to have moved into premises previously used as a second office by a partner who had retired.

We also have data for twelve firms which moved within the area, from one set of premises to another. Three were shops, six were offices, two were industry and one was a warehouse. Three had left their former premises because of clearance actions, two because of business expansion, one because of traffic problems, and one because the building was in bad condition and the landlord was unwilling to do repairs. This last occupier also complained that the rent and rates of the former premises had risen. Eight of these firms employed fewer than five persons, while four employed between five and nine persons.

It was very difficult for us to trace the emigrant firms. Often even the Board of Trade had no idea where they had gone. In all there were one hundred of them, but in two cases the firms concerned had occupied more than one set of premises in the area and had then decided to close down one of their branches. Another firm occupying two premises had closed both. Allowing for these cases we have ninety-seven firms who had left the area, possibly to go somewhere else, or possibly to close down. Their distribution between land-uses and their sizes are shown in Table 5.

It will be noticed that two-thirds of the firms leaving the area employed fewer than five persons, while three-quarters of them had

TABLE 5. LAND-USE AND SIZE OF 97 FIRMS LEAVING THE AREA

Land-use		Size by number of employees	
Shopping	21	0–4 persons	63
Office	40	5–9 persons	13
Industry	24	10–19 persons	6
Warehousing	10	20–49 persons	2
Residential hostel	1	50 and over	2
Public assembly	1	unclassified	11

fewer than ten employees. These ratios do not appear to differ substantially from 1962 size-distribution of firms.

The slight change in the size-distribution of firms between 1962 and 1964 is due more to the inflow of slightly larger established firms than to the exodus of smaller firms.

One may look similarly at the changes in land-use. As a net result of inward and outward movement the number of offices increased by eleven, while shops declined by six, industrial establishments by twenty-three, and warehouses by nine. The balance of the area thus changed considerably.

Of the ninety-seven emigrant firms, we were able to trace only twenty-four. Of these nineteen replied to our inquiry about reasons for moving.

Two were shops selling motor vehicles or components. They had moved because of increased rents. One, which had been there since 1919 and employed between ten and nineteen people, also complained of parking problems.

Seven office tenants were traced. Four of these had moved into central Manchester, two because they wanted to expand, one in a desire to contract, and one because of parking and traffic problems. Similar reasons were given by the three who moved elsewhere.

The five industrial land-users who gave reasons for emigrating had all moved into the area during the war or earlier. The main reasons for moving out of it were a desire to expand (in two cases), rising rents (in another two cases, including one which also gave parking problems as a main reason) and clearance. Parking and traffic problems were frequent subsidiary reasons.

The other firms giving information had warehouses. One moved out because of clearance action. The other two gave parking and traffic problems as main reasons and listed rent increases as subsidiary reasons. One of these listed as a main reason the fact that the area was declining and no longer suitable.

More detailed information is given in Appendix 3. In looking at it one may note the frequency with which the main reason for moving involved either clearance or the fact that the building or site was now too small. The most frequently cited subsidiary reasons concerned parking and unloading. We shall refer to these points when we develop our theory.

We had hoped to be able to say something about the probability of a firm's moving. If we had had more data we might have found that a firm of land-use *X* and size *Y* which had been in the area for *Z* years would be more likely to move than one of a different description. Possibly, too, we could have produced a ranking of reasons for moving. Unfortunately, despite a great deal of effort, we failed to get the data. Our attempt to find a statistical description of the footloose firm had to be abandoned. If we had kept a frequent check on tenancies and detected moves rather earlier, we might have been successful.

It is, once again, the paucity of data that prevents us from feeling very happy about generalisations of such ideas as we have about what factors are important in causing people to move. For all that, we have learned something about a specific area, and the experience gained from its study has helped us to think about the wider issues.

As one reads this account of the movement of firms, one cannot help noticing the frequent references to traffic. Few firms can fulfil their functions without it, yet in comments on urban decay there seems to be more concern about the way in which excessive or ill-organised traffic may cause environmental decay than about the way in which inadequate traffic facilities may lead to tenant obsolescence and hence to physical decay.

As part of our study we looked at the movements of one kind of traffic—goods vehicles. The analysis was undertaken by J. B. McLoughlin, who is responsible for this part of this chapter.

The quality of the replies was not high, and our conclusions must be viewed very cautiously. In some cases the occupier provided no information. In other cases the reply was ambiguous or incomplete. Because of this our analysis sometimes has been based partly on assumptions about the meaning of an ambiguous reply or the probable amount of trip-generation. These have influenced our diagrams, but not our statistical computations. Our conclusions must be interpreted simply as being indicative of hypotheses that may be worth further investigation.

Information on trips* made by staffs or by customers and other callers at premises was almost absent. Much fuller information was found on trips made for the purposes of bringing goods to premises (e.g. raw materials, components, faulty goods for repair, stocks for retailers, etc.) or despatching goods from premises. There was a total of over 650 survey cards, of which more than 200 des-

---

* Throughout this, note the term 'trips' refers to *an outward and return journey combined.*

cribed firms that had regular movements of goods. After having discarded all those cards with manifest inaccuracies or ambiguities beyond resolution, there remained 103 cards suitable for analysis.

Three main analyses were made:

(a) Trips in relation to location of premises within the survey area.

(b) Trips in relation to land-use.

(c) Trips in relation to floor-space.

The first outstanding characteristic of the area revealed by a study of this data was that of concentration of the trip-generators along the major streets. This is particularly marked along Deansgate and to a lesser extent along Quay Street–Peter Street, Liverpool Road and Whitworth Street West. By contrast, minor streets—Byrom Street, St John Street, Tonman Street, Watson Street, etc.—hardly figure at all as the locations of trip termini.

This state of affairs is in direct conflict with the need to segregate primary traffic movements from those associated with goods delivery and other movements involving direct access to buildings. Deansgate, for example, is serving as a primary traffic route to and within central Manchester, as well as giving direct, mostly kerbside, access to a great many buildings.

Such a marked pattern could scarcely have arisen by chance, and it seemed reasonable to suppose that one explanation might be that in the process of 'colonisation' of the study area, those activities requiring the most frequent deliveries by goods vehicles tended to congregate along the principal frontages and to remain there. Accordingly this supposition was tested by mapping the locations of all firms by duration of stay in the area. The supposition was found to be confirmed; Figure 13 shows the locations of firms that arrived in the area before 1930 and between 1930 and 1944. The concentration along Deansgate and especially around the Quay Street–Peter Street intersection is very marked. Figure 14 shows arrivals between 1945 and 1957 and firms who have entered in 1958 and later. There is still a remarkable concentration along Deansgate, but a certain 'scattering' westwards towards Byrom Street is evident, as is the line-up along the southern frontage of Liverpool Road.

A further concentration of the survey material suggested *prima facie* that those activities occupying the smaller floor-areas might be concentrated in a similar fashion, and this indeed proved to be so.

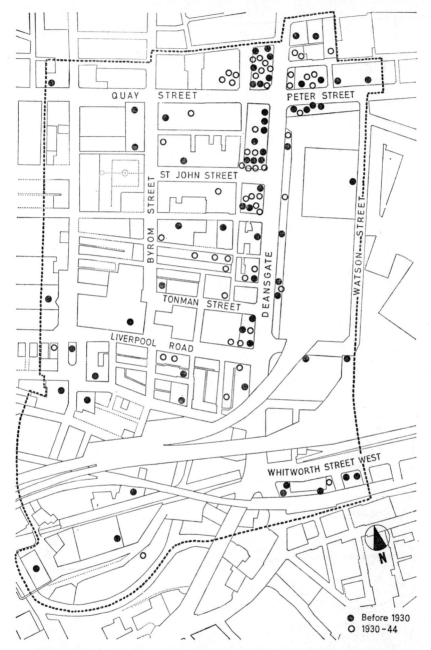

Figure 13. Firms that moved into the Lower Deansgate study area before 1945

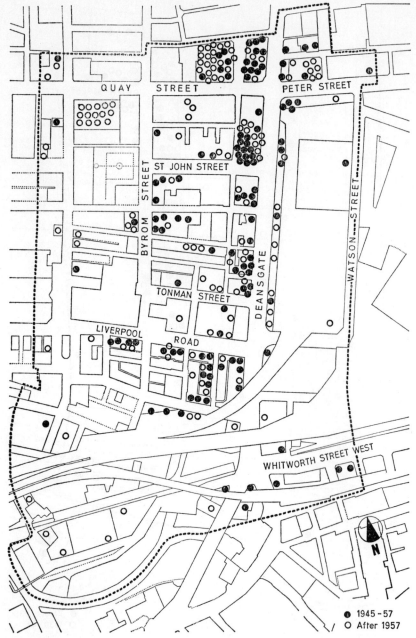

Figure 14. Firms that moved into the Lower Deansgate study area after 1944

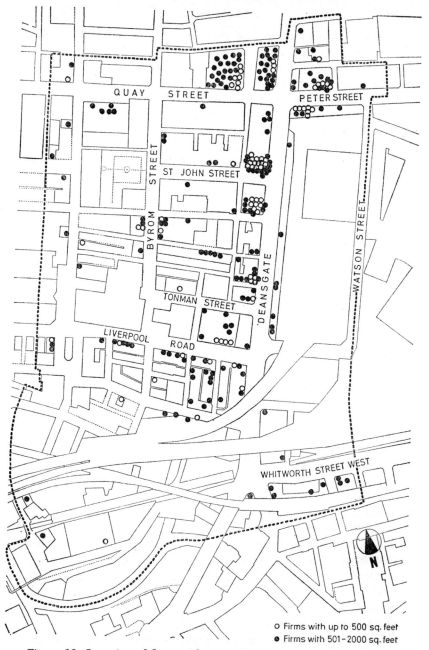

Figure 15. Location of firms with up to 2000 square feet in the Lower Deansgate study area

○ Firms with up to 500 sq. feet
● Firms with 501-2000 sq. feet

QUAY STREET
PETER STREET
ST JOHN STREET
BYROM STREET
WATSON STREET
DEANSGATE
TONMAN STREET
LIVERPOOL ROAD
WHITWORTH STREET WEST
N

Figure 15 shows that firms of less than 2000 square feet floor-area, and especially those with less than 500 square feet are similarly concentrated along the western frontage of Deansgate (and markedly around the Peter Street–Quay Street crossing) with a subsidiary alignment along Liverpool Road. Figure 16 shows how the firms with larger floor-areas tend to be more evenly spread throughout the area. To some extent this may reflect the secular trend in business towards the larger unit operating nationally or regionally and also the relative difficulty experienced by the later arrivals in acquiring main frontages compared with 'backland' sites, some of which have been made available by clearance of substandard housing under the Housing Acts. (See Figure 14—arrivals 1945 and later.)

Our next analysis looked at the relationships between the total of inward and outward trips per thousand square feet of floor-area and the land-use. For this we used both 1961 and 1964 data. The main results are shown in Table 6.

The 1964 survey material for traffic is based on an analysis of only 28 items and may be regarded as statistically inadequate. The 1961 material is derived from a study of 103 items, the selection of which has already been discussed. Even though there is almost four times the number of 1964 items it is very doubtful if much weight can be given to the figures themselves as guides to more general conditions. One must be content with drawing out only the broadest indications and using these as pointers towards the possible results of wider studies based on more accurate original data for a greater number of items.

One might thus instance the markedly higher rates of goods vehicles trip-generation (1961 data) among the retail and office land-uses in general compared with the lower figures for storage and industrial uses. This observation, together with that noted earlier concerning the concentration of trip-generations along the main street frontages, hinted at a possible relationship between the rate of trip-generation (per unit floor-area) and the floor-area itself. One marked, and measurable, characteristic difference between different land-uses is the wide divergence of floor-areas. Storage and retail uses illustrate this. In an attempt to test the hypothesis, we correlated the trips made by goods vehicles with the floor-area. We give some detail of our calculations in Appendix 4.

There would seem to be some slight correlation between goods trips and floor-areas, but it is also evident that factors other than

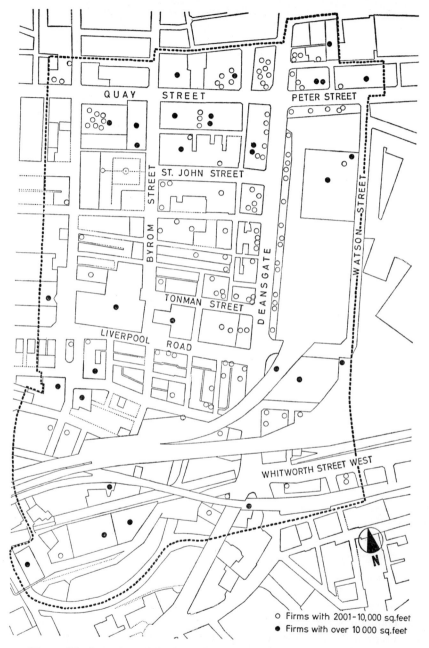

Figure 16. Location of firms with more than 2000 square feet in the
Lower Deansgate study area

QUAY STREET
PETER STREET
ST. JOHN STREET
BYROM STREET
WATSON STREET
DEANSGATE
TONMAN STREET
LIVERPOOL ROAD
WHITWORTH STREET WEST
N

o Firms with 2001–10,000 sq.feet
● Firms with over 10 000 sq.feet

TABLE 6. TRIPS PER 1000 SQUARE FEET, BY LAND-USE, IN LOWER DEANSGATE SURVEY

Land-use code	Description	Trips per week per 1000 sq. ft.	
		1961	*1964*
00	Grocers: baker/confect., sweets/tobac., butcher, fishmonger; greengrocer, flowers, wines, etc.	47·4	1·60
01	Restaurants, cafés	10·8	—
02	Public houses	1·9	—
03	Draper/furrier; outfitters, shoes	4·2	—
07	Consumer durables, radio-TV-records, paints, office equipment	13·5	51·0
08	Motors, motor cycles, parts, components, accessories	9·8	—
09	Dry-cleaners, pawnbrokers, betting, hairdressing, tickets	—	70·8
12	Insurance offices	—	20·0
14	Accountants' offices	—	9·3
15	Company offices	20·0	30·9
16	Professional services	—	11·1
17	Central and local government offices	13·5	—
18	Business services, agencies, etc.	11·6	—
19	Miscellaneous offices	2·9	98·0
30	Libraries	13·6	—
33	Hospitals/clinics	9·0	—
37	Clubs, assembly hall, etc.	1·2	—
40	Manufacturing industry	5·3	2·1
41	Service industry	10·6	14·5
70	Wholesale warehouse	4·3	12·6
71	Storage warehouse or space	8·6	—
72	Open-air storage	1·0	—

those considered here play a part. The evidence is inconclusive, but common sense does suggest that the users of large floor-areas are necessarily more concerned about, and skilled in, the organisation not only of space *within* buildings, but also of *vehicular movements*

between them, and that the smaller firms, being relatively uncon-
cerned about the use of large, expensive spaces or about the organisation of goods transport would tend to be greater trip-generators
per unit of floor-area. Larger users may also possess larger vehicles
or order in greater bulk.

The smaller floor-areas, as we have seen, tend to be occupied by
the quick-turnover retail trades, which require more frequent trips
for the replenishment of stocks (restaurants, cafés, grocers, etc.)
and removal of 'empties' than do the wholesalers and storage firms
occupying large spaces and often perhaps employing skilled transport managers and using their *own* transport more efficiently.

It seems that this study has confirmed the widely held view that
main roads are all too often lined with the premises of firms whose
activities are among the highest traffic-generators, while the 'backland' is devoted to occupants who are relatively under-demanding
of loading and unloading time and space. In this area Deansgate
pre-eminently, and the other main routes to a lesser extent, suffer
considerably because their frontages are high trip-generators,
loading and unloading being done from the kerbside in the great
majority of cases. One might tentatively suggest that from the goods
traffic point of view, one goal of redevelopment policy and planning
action might be an attempt to turn the area 'inside out' i.e. to remove
the high trip-generators from the main frontages and to concentrate
them in the 'backland', leaving the main streets for movement and
keeping the servicing of buildings away from them.

Two other aspects of traffic and decay are illustrated by recent
events in Exeter. The removal of a bus station led to a change in the
direction of pedestrian traffic, and so to declining trade for certain
shops. Their strategic locational advantage disappeared, profits
declined and the buildings ceased to be the most suitable for their
function. The shopkeepers moved out, rents fell and eventually the
state of decay was reached. Had the bus station remained, many of
these buildings would still be in reasonable repair, or possibly they
would have been redeveloped. This does not mean that it was wrong
to move the bus station, but it does illustrate the way in which a
decision of this kind may lead to decay in one place while bringing
growth to another.

In the same city, one of the main shopping streets has until
recently had car-parking on both sides. This slowed down the flow
of traffic along that particular road, which happened to lead directly

into the centre (the High Street is a continuation of it), where congestion was very severe. This means that a certain slowness in this
street was not very important, because most of the traffic met its real
bottleneck farther along, where the road narrowed. But the traders
of this street relied heavily on the 'drive, stop and buy' trade, which
could be attracted only if cars could stop for twenty minutes or so.
This was forbidden on most of one side. It may be argued that
Exeter had rather special traffic problems, and that the net consequences of this action were in some sense advantageous to the
community. If this is argued, then the loss of trade and the probable
acceleration of decay must figure in the balance sheet.

The impact of parking restrictions on shops and other forms of
business is a matter that has been inadequately considered. A small
study recently conducted at the University of Manchester Centre
for Urban and Regional Research sheds a little light upon it. A
suburban area of Manchester containing mixed land-uses, including
959 shops, was examined. Parking restrictions had been introduced
between 1961 and 1966 along the frontages of 181 of these shops. By
using rating registers it was possible to count the numbers of changes
of tenancy in various periods, and the duration during which a shop
was empty. The results are of some interest.

In the year leading up to the introduction of parking restrictions
there were 8 tenancy changes amongst the 59 affected shops, compared with 47 amongst 348 unaffected shops. In the year following
the date of restrictions, there were 12 tenancy changes in the
restricted area and 55 in the unrestricted area. This evidence does not
significantly indicate any greater tendency for shops to become vacant
when parking restrictions are introduced.

When the periods of observation were lengthened to two years
before and after the introduction of restrictions a similar result
emerged. But when we looked at the period for which a shop remained empty the story was different. In the two years before the restrictions the average period of emptiness was 44·9 days in the unrestricted area and 54·9 days in the restricted streets. In the two years
following the introduction of restrictions the average periods of
emptiness were 57·7 and 95·8 days respectively. This is a highly
significant result, indicating that while in this area the introduction of
parking restrictions did not increase the chance of a shop becoming
empty, it certainly did mean that an empty shop was likely to stay
empty for much longer. And empty property breeds decay.

CHAPTER 5

The Analysis of Urban Change

We have emphasised that urban decay is a natural process that we can to some extent control and use. If this is to be done without risk of our creating a situation worse than that which would have occurred without our intervention, we need to understand the ways in which various forces propel the changing town. The empirical work reported in chapters 2–4 helps us to do this, but we also need a sound theory of urban change, compatible with our empirical findings and more general observations. Only when we have this will we be able to locate the important gaps in our knowledge and to appreciate the full extent of the possible consequences of our actions. This chapter is intended as a contribution to such a theory. Because our main aim is to pave the way for a policy towards urban decay, we will not attempt to summarise many other theories of urban development. Instead we shall suggest a theoretical framework that will be capable of supporting further analysis, yet, as it stands, be useful to the policy-maker.

Our analysis falls into three parts. There is a micro-analysis, in which we are concerned with individual buildings or small groups of them. Here we examine the decisions that lead to decay, maintenance or redevelopment. Then we consider a macro-analysis, in which we study the forces that mould the shape of the town and determine its land-use pattern. Finally we suggest a different kind of analysis, involving urban-simulation models, and argue that this is the best way to integrate our micro- and macro-analyses so that they may be useful at the design and policy levels.

We may begin by summarising the main empirical findings reported in chapters 2–4. The first findings concern the Manchester area and may not be true elsewhere.

1. Urban locations with buildings tend to have a worse environment (as defined for our index) than urban locations remote from buildings.

2. At the level of the individual building there is no particular association between the outward appearance of the building and the quality of its environment.

3. When larger areas are considered, there appears to be a significant positive correlation between the average condition of the buildings in the area, and the average state of the environment; but this seems to be true only when a certain stage of decay has been reached. For less decayed areas there is no significant association with environmental quality.

4. The outward appearance of houses (as measured by our index) is closely associated with their internal adequacy (as measured by the census of population data).

5. Physical decay declines as we move outwards from the centre of Manchester.

6. As the proportion of owner-occupiers rises, the severity of decay declines and the environment improves.

7. Overcrowding—but not multi-tenancy of a kind that does not lead to overcrowding—is associated with decay and bad environment.

8. Densely built residential areas are more likely to be highly decayed.

9. Environmental decay decreases with distance from the centre of the town and is highly correlated with the lack of the exclusive use of domestic facilities.

10. Age may be the link that explains several of the above correlations.

11. Slum 'residual' areas tend to have above-average numbers of young families and young children.

12. These areas tend to have high-fertility rates, but comparatively fewer females per thousand males. These factors may reflect low incomes.

13. These areas also have a high proportion of widowed, divorced or single heads of households.

14. Slum 'transitional' areas have a more varied social class structure than residual areas.

15. Juvenile crime is more common in the residual areas than in transitional areas.

16. Health disorders, child-neglect and illegitimacy are more common in downtown transitional areas.

17. In the commercial twilight zone of Lower Deansgate, offices

tended to be in better condition than did the shops, which were better than industrial premises.

18. Office tenants were often new to the area and were there because of central-area redevelopment. They were more inclined to improve their properties than were shopkeepers.

19. Shopkeepers were less likely to be new tenants and were attracted by low rents, almost-central location and the existence of a nucleus of similar or complementary shops.

20. Trade in one area may benefit from parking restrictions elsewhere: and this may lead to a search for larger premises.

21. It is allegedly easier to obtain female labour in areas where there are shops.

22. Areas that are quiet at night may be prone to burglary.

23. Planning uncertainties lead to difficulties for occupiers of business premises.

24. Firms are most likely to move because of rising rents, un-adaptability of the premises or parking and other traffic problems.

25. If a given floor-space is occupied by few users, it is likely to generate fewer trips than if it is subdivided between more users.

26. Main roads tend to be lined with high traffic-generators.

27. Parking restrictions may sometimes lead to loss of trade and/or to premises being empty for lengthy periods.

We must, of course, keep in mind that almost all of these 'conclusions' are based on only very limited studies; and that possibly they do not hold in other places, or might even not always hold in the areas studied. There is need for much more investigation. Yet it is difficult to read this list of findings, even with this caution in mind, without being tempted to construct some theory that may help to unite them. We shall start with a theory concerning individual buildings.

We have already hinted at some of the ways in which decay may arise, and referred to the fact that it could arise simply because the income derived from the building was insufficient to pay maintenance-costs. Now we must consider these ideas in more detail. We must also relate decay more precisely than we have yet done to the whole process of urban change, and to public and private investment.

Hitherto most towns have developed through the aggregation of thousands of individual decisions by citizens, usually taken with little knowledge or consideration of the future decisions currently being evolved by others and with little regard to the consequences on the community of the development concerned. The motives have been various: sometimes private profit or convenience; sometimes in recent years philanthropy or concern for public welfare and the under-privileged; sometimes vote-catching. Whether development has been privately or publicly sponsored, a dominant consideration has been that there should be quick, and preferably obvious, returns on the investment of funds. While private developers have sometimes taken a fairly long view, public development has often been dictated by a policy of expediency. Consequently the long-term impact of development on the community, as opposed to an individual, a firm, or that part of the community that is nearest to the development, has too rarely been considered.[1] Yet buildings last for a very long term.

Where a large part of a town was built in a short time, as in the case of Manchester or Middlesbrough,[2] there is likely to be a more concentrated renewal problem than if the original pace of development had been slower. A large upsurge in building, such as occurred in most British towns in the decade centred on 1870,[3] is to have some echo today in the demand for renewal. If all buildings last equally well before entering a stage of recognisable decay, then the shape of the graph showing buildings constructed over time would be accurately reproduced some generations later in the graph of buildings becoming decayed. As it is, however, the durability of buildings varies, and therefore the echo effect is diffused. Some houses built in 1870 were in need of replacement twenty years ago; others still show no sign of decay. The actual life of a building depends upon its natural life, and on the timing and adequacy of maintenance and adaptation expenditures, which in turn depend upon the adaptability of the original design and all those forces that may lead to functional obsolescence. Unfortunately we still tend to ignore the impact of functional change.[4]

We are also too prone to forget that just as there is variability in the natural life of buildings, so there is a spread of actual life-spans. The tendency here is to look at the life of existing buildings, and to work out either some average or some maximum.[5] A more interesting procedure would be to take a sample of the local authority building-registers for, say, 1860–3 and for similar periods at decennial intervals.[6] From these one could select a sample of buildings and discover whether they still exist. The same registers would be a useful supplement to legal deeds and other sources consulted to determine when buildings were demolished. From those data one could then construct life-tables for buildings erected in 1860–3, in 1870–3, and so on. Unfortunately nothing like this has yet been done.[7]

Because there has been no useful empirical work in Britain on the impact of functional obsolescence on the lifetime of a building, or even on the distributions of actual lives around a mean, we are not yet in a position to test theories relating to these subjects, or to evaluate with any confidence the probable consequences of many building decisions.[8] The analysis that follows must therefore rest on assumptions that we will not always be able to substantiate, except by reference to isolated examples and to the findings we have just listed.

Building decay, functional obsolescence and environmental decay are closely interwoven. Each may be caused independently of the others, but each may also lead to either, or both, of the others. A decaying building may become inappropriate to its function because it weakens, fails to protect its occupants from the weather, creates a bad impression upon its occupants, their friends or their customers, or fails to conform with changing legal requirements. It may lead to environmental decay because untidiness tends to breed untidiness, or indirectly because in its decaying state it now accommodates a different function.

Functional obsolescence may lead to building decay if it provides an income insufficient for financing repairs, or for keeping the building heated and ventilated. It may cause environmental decay by encouraging building decay. Alternatively it may do so because the new function is a less tidy one, or generates a different kind or volume of traffic or is of a lower prestige and so encourages neighbouring tenants to move.

Environmental decay can clearly cause some occupiers to consider that the location is no longer suitable, however good the building may be. This can lead to vacancies or lowered rents, and so to building decay.

Because of these interdependencies, and, in particular, the impact of environmental decay on building decay, any attempt to predict the actual life of a specified building has to be in the context of its function and location, and has to include consideration of the probable lives of neighbouring buildings. One has also to consider the possibility of the building being demolished before it has reached any advanced stage of decay. It should be possible to assemble some evidence about the probabilities of various states of decay or change of function leading to other states, according to the detail of the case, by spending sufficient time and money on field studies in appropriate areas. Until this is done we may be able to obtain some insight through the use of simulation models and guesswork.

The rather vaguely quantified relationship between building activity some generations ago and current renewal problems, stemming from both natural decay and the modifications to this due to other factors means that many towns that grew rapidly and prosperously at some time in the last century are now in need of almost complete renewal at a time when they are no longer prosperous. The problem has been aggravated by the almost complete cessation of new building and all but urgent maintenance-work during the war. As a consequence, when the war ended, the housing shortage discouraged demolition, while the housing drive made maintenance-work difficult or expensive at a time when rent control was keeping income from property at a level that often did not cover the cost of repairs. As time has gone on, the housing shortage has eased, and all buildings have become older. This has made it both possible and necessary for the Government to show more active concern about renewal than it has in the past. Had there been no housing shortage after the war, and had reasonable maintenance continued, it would have been possible almost twenty years ago to begin a more gradual renewal. Our position today arises from the fact that at a time when the buildings erected between 1850 and 1900 were beginning to need substantial attention or replacement, the war and its aftermath prevented us from facing up to the task. To what extent half a century of rent control has added to the deterioration of our buildings we cannot say.

The compression of renewal demand into the later part of the period during which it might more naturally have arisen has made the problems facing any local authority, and especially those small ones that grew rapidly last century, much more acute. Here, very often, are towns that no longer have a prosperous industrial *raison d'être*, but have a low rateable value and are faced with a physical disintegration of fabric. This is but one of the many factors causing reassessment of both the rating system and local-authority boundaries. Another is the problem of the large city whose more prosperous residents are now technically in a different local authority just beyond its boundaries. Such a city has a depleted income out of which to pay for a growing renewal or clearance programme.

This rather broad discussion of the origins of decay is adequate for some purposes, but it does not provide us with a real understanding of the forces at work, and so we cannot, either, understand the function of decay. We may begin to do so if we look at an economic theory of urban decay, describing a simplified town in which all buildings are rented, by their owners, to tenants.[9] Briefly, this theory begins by distinguishing between different kinds of obsolescence. We may suppose that when a tenant first enters a building he decides that of the buildings currently available to him this particular one suits his purpose as well as any other, after making allowance for the rent. He chooses it out of several possibilities. With the passing of time he may feel that for all sorts of reasons it is no longer the most suitable of the buildings available to him. Perhaps his family has altered in size or his business in size and kind. Perhaps his customers look differently upon its location than they did. Possibly it is no longer in an adequate state of repair. His income or neighbours may have changed. These are but some of the reasons. The important point is that the tenant no longer considers its occupation to be his best course. The occupation of the building becomes—for that tenant—obsolete. We once referred to this as a state of *tenant obsolescence*, although if we were evolving the theory now we might refer to it as *functional obsolescence*. It is in order to perform some function that the tenant occupies a building. However, the earlier phrase has its use because it emphasises the dependency of this obsolescence upon a single occupier. Possibly, when the building is vacated, a new tenant wishing to perform exactly the same kind of function will come along. He may choose to occupy the building because the function is on a different scale, because he has different rates of substitution between convenience and money, or even because, given exactly the same facts and tastes, he may reach different conclusions than the other man. Thus tenant obsolescence need not imply functional obsolescence unless this is defined in narrow personal terms.

The building has another purpose besides that generated by its user. This is to provide the owner with an income. To avoid confusion we will not refer to this as a function. The landlord has to decide whether he is making the most of his assets. Can he, by altering the rent of the existing building, make more money? If so, would it be by raising or by lowering the rent? If the building is often empty, he could achieve his purpose by the latter alternative. We refer to the state of affairs that exists when the landlord feels that the existing rent agreement is obsolete as one of *rental obsolescence*. This may be *upward* or *downward*, according to whether the rent should be raised or lowered. Upward rental obsolescence is irrelevant where there is rent control.

He may feel that it would be profitable to spend some money on the building, possibly because this would enable him to charge a higher rent or to continue to draw a rent that at present is threatened. His best course of action is not to leave the condition of the building as it is. This is the state of *condition obsolescence*.

Three other possibilities are of interest to us. Perhaps the landlord will feel that the most profitable thing to do is to demolish the building and to use the site for another purpose—possibly for a modern but otherwise similar building, or for some other kind of building or even for no building at all. We shall refer to this as a state of *building obsolescence*.

Another possibility for us to consider is that in which the most profitable thing to do is to spend nothing on the maintenance of the building even after physical deterioration has set in, and even if this leads to tenant obsolescence or downward rental obsolescence. We refer to this, within the context of this theory, as the *state of decay*. Clearly it implies that the landlord can see no more profitable alternative than that of letting the building rot.

Keeping these definitions in mind, suppose that because of, say, traffic conditions, tenant obsolescence sets in and the tenant leaves as soon as he can. The landlord considers what is profitable. If the demand for occupation of the building is high, he may decide that there is upward rental obsolescence. Alternatively he may decide that the demand for occupation of the site is so high that there is building obsolescence.

At the other extreme, when demand for occupation of the building is low, lie various possibilities. If at the same time demand for occupation of the site is high, then condition obsolescence or building obsolescence is indicated. If, on the other hand, neither the building nor the site is very popular, then possibly it is still a case of condition obsolescence, but more probably the answer lies in downward rental obsolescence. This is never a happy thought, as it implies that the landlord has to content himself with a lower income than he once expected. Perhaps, even then, he will have also to accept decay, for repairs are beyond his means.

Other examples of the links between these different kinds of obsolescence are given elsewhere.[10] What we have to notice here is that both the dating and the type of obsolescence are dependent upon many factors. If a building boom results in the more or less simultaneous granting of many leases for identical periods, then towards the expiry of this period both the tenant and the owners will be faced with decisions. The longer the lease, the greater the opportunity for change, not only in the condition of the building, but also in its functional suitability and in the demand for occupation of the building or the site. If all the leases have been granted for, say, fifty years, then substantial decay may appear after about forty years, either because of downward rental obsolescence following tenant obsolescence, or because as soon as the lease ends there will be upward rental obsolescence or building obsolescence. The owner may feel that by allowing the building to begin to decay he may accelerate the termination of the lease, and so be able to improve his property and to let it at a higher rent all the sooner. Alternatively he may feel that maintenance is not worth while if he is going to redevelop within a few years. To some extent both of these possibilities arise because of the landlord's inability to vary the rent during the life of the lease. When short leases are granted, there are more opportunities for decision, and it is easier to keep the rent abreast with current demand and supply. Both decay and redevelopment are spread over longer periods, partly because changes can occur after, say, fourteen, twenty-one or twenty-eight years, instead of after fifty, and partly because the opportunities for rent increase that offset rising maintenance-costs, and so discourage decay, are more frequent.

For a given building the granting of a long lease with no rent-adjustment clause and inadequate insistence on proper maintenance seems likely to accelerate decay, unless the building is so defective or so unfortunately sited that only the long lease keeps it tenanted. We have just argued that the simultaneous granting of many long leases can thus lead to a wave of decay and redevelopment. But if development has been gradual, over forty or fifty years (and so far as we can tell this never has been the case in any country),[11] then long leases may be socially useful by preventing a large number of tenants or landlords from simultaneously responding to some change,

in a way that they could if there were simply renewable short-term leases.

Other factors affecting the timing and type of obsolescence are all of those that may lead to functional obsolescence (among which we must include transport changes and environmental obsolescence), those which lead to changes in demand for a site, and those relating to the costs of maintenance and new building. We must keep in mind, too, that expectations of what may happen can be more important than what does happen.

It is sometimes suggested that one way of preventing decay is to build adaptable buildings, so that as functions change the buildings may be altered to accommodate them. There is probably much truth in this idea: but it has to be regarded with some caution. The transitional areas, described by Miss Gittus in Chapter 3, have assumed their characteristics largely because of the ease with which large family houses have been adapted into staircases of bed-sitters. There is no one cause of, or cure for, functional obsolescence.

In this treatment we have, of course, simplified the story by assuming that the building-owner is also the ground landlord. It can be argued that in effect he is, since the building-owner is normally required to surrender the building in fair condition to the ground landlord when the lease expires. On the other hand, the building-owner can sometimes sub-let for short leases. This means that he has opportunity to adjust the rents to maintenance-costs and to demand conditions. Given this, upward rental obsolescence and condition obsolescence are more likely than they would be with long sub-leases. What the building-owner who is not also the ground landlord cannot normally do, without consent, is to redevelop. If, however, this seems profitable to him, it may also be profitable to the ground landlord, and a new lease can be negotiated. He should not, according to his lease, let the building decay: but often he does, partly because he believes that he can get away with it.

From the landlord's point of view, decay means a depreciation of income-earning assets. It compels him to reassess his prospects, and may draw his attention to the fact that he is not making the most profitable use of his site. This is an important and often forgotten function.

There is, however, another kind of obsolescence, which can occur when both the tenant and the landlord are perfectly happy. This is obsolescence from the broader viewpoint of a community. Even though the community neither owns nor rents a site, the use to which it is put can have economic consequences for others. Any land-use generating an economic activity is bound, of course, to have its wider consequences: but these will depend on the location of the site as well as on the activity itself. A time could come when the representatives of the community might feel it advantageous to move an occupier to another site, paying him and the landowner compensation for having to move.

This *community obsolescence* can (but need not) lead to decay. If, for example, the community felt so strongly about the obsolete private use of a site that it deprived the occupier of public services or created a refuse dump next door to it, then downward rental obsolescence could set in. Usually, however, a sale would be effected before this stage. The way in which community obsolescence is more likely to lead to decay is through the publication of long-term planning ideas, which so affect the expectations of owners, occupiers and speculators that in many cases buildings become empty or ill maintained just as they may often be redeveloped. A vague plan, indicating that a new main road will pass somewhere through an area, can lead to an extensive decay. Sometimes it means that the local authority can eventually acquire the property much more cheaply than if it had been more specific in its proposals and more speedy in their implementation.

Community obsolescence of one site—such as the removal of a bus station, which leads to the transference of an activity to another site—can lead to a functional obsolescence on neighbouring sites and so eventually to a downward rental obsolescence and decay. This kind of community obsolescence may arise because either the site is not being put to its 'best' use, or the activity on it is not on its 'best' location. In the former case there is a parallel to building obsolescence, while the latter parallels tenant or functional obsolescence.

Sometimes community obsolescence of a seemingly different kind arises. An example is the case of Wells, where a city of purely ecclesiastical function, with consequent market activities, has reached a stage where, despite some modern industry and a useful tourist trade, there are signs of stagnation of a kind that can lead to declining population. The ancient function of the local community can no longer support a city of this size, with costs at current levels, while the newer functions have not reached either the diversity or the intensity that is required. Here possibly is an argument, not necessarily convincing, for endowing places like Wells with complementary institutional functions, such as universities or other educational establishments. How well a business school could thrive in Buxton, where the businessmen could retreat a little from the bustle of a big city, yet, if the school were large enough, still have all the advantages of a university. At the same time the town would acquire a new and growing function. These remarks are, of course, a digression, but they underline another source of decay, and indicate one way of injecting a new vigour into communities that have dying functions.

Jargon has no place unless it clarifies. The terms we have just used help us to understand, and to talk about, some of the many changes that we place under the umbrella of obsolescence. One conclusion that emerges from this discussion is that if *community building obsolescence* (as described above) coincides with decay, then the scene is set for redevelopment. If it coincides with downward rental obsolescence, then perhaps decay can be forestalled, at the cost of a higher purchase price. If decay precedes community obsolescence, there may be a case for subsidy. From the community's point of view, decay has the function of facilitating or cheapening the public acquisition of land, and so presenting opportunities for planned development. Even so the opportunity is not complete if money, men and materials are not available, while it is of little use if the community lacks a long-term plan. In particular it is of little use if a community has to think narrowly, within the context of boundaries or annual budgets that compel it to plan the maximisation of rateable income rather than for a more efficient or beautiful or otherwise desirable use of land. Joseph Chamberlain estimated in 1876 that it would cost Birmingham Corporation £1,310,000 to acquire forty-three derelict acres. The building of new streets to relieve central traffic problems would cost money and take up land. From the rest an income could be derived, which had to be set against loan charges spread over fifty years. The annual cost to the Corporation would be £18,000, but increased rateable value could be deducted from this, to reduce the cost to £12,000 per annum. This would be about £50,000–£60,000 at today's prices.

'Is that too heavy a burden for the town of Birmingham to contemplate?' he asked. 'I believe the Town, and, above all, the next generation will have cause to bless the Town Council if it . . . exercises what I venture to call a sagacious audacity.'

Yet when his son proposed a similar scheme in Birmingham in 1907, he failed, as it would have added one halfpenny in the pound to the rates. In the words of an unknown ratepayer: 'My grandfather did not spend five-twelfths of his income for my benefit, and I for one would strongly object to paying eight shillings and four-pence in the pound rates for the benefit of posterity.'[12]

Perhaps the greatest advantage of the cost–benefit techniques now being evolved is that they make us more aware of the benefits we may be creating for our own generation, as well as for posterity.

But we must return to our theory. So far we have shown how a wide range of economic, social, legal, institutional or technical changes may impel the user of a building to decide that it is no longer the most suitable place for him, and may persuade the owner that he should change his assessment of the best thing to do. We have also seen how this may involve changes in rent and in the environment. Chapter 3 presents arguments relating these changes and subdivision of tenancies to social changes. What we must now do is to look at the town in rather wider terms, in which the individual building is too small to play a part.

A town is more than a collection of houses. It contains shops, offices, schools and other forms of industry and service. Within are communal ties, some purely social and others dependent upon trading. Its pattern of land-use has emerged over a period of many years, rarely as the result of even a countable set of identifiable decisions, but almost always through a long sequence of actions, some private and some public, some accidental and some deliberate, taken only when the opportunity has existed, and often based on contradictory criteria.

Most of our towns have developed in an unplanned way, growing to sizes far exceeding those contemplated by the people whose separate or collective decisions established the basic form of their centres several generations ago. There is no need here to attempt even an outline of the growth and development of our mostly centre-orientated towns from these early beginnings. It is enough for us to make two observations. One is that the pattern of land-use that has emerged from countless decisions in the past is not necessarily that which best suits the requirements of a larger group of people, having and developing different standards, and using different forms of transport. The second is that while we can plan new towns according to modern principles and experiment with different urban forms, we are still so ill-informed about the forces at work in a town that there is a great danger that in solving some problems we may be creating others quite as bad.

A town centre is a meeting-place. In some towns there are several distinct centres, devoted to shopping, commerce, entertainment and other functions. This is particularly likely to be true of the larger towns, and in these there may be several centres, each devoted to some of these functions. Continuing in this way, one could define the centre of the town in terms of its functions, but there is another approach to its definition. This is in terms of journeys made by people. If one were to record all of the trips made by the residents of a town during a week, describing the home as the origin and the other end of the trip as the destination, then in many towns the zones with the highest number of destinations per unit area could reasonably be called the centre. This would probably be so in most towns if one omitted those trips that are essentially journeys to work. In omitting these trips one would, of course, be omitting many that go to the centre. There would remain trips for shopping, business, personal services and pleasure. All of these involve meeting other people.

We begin with these parallel approaches to the town centre, in terms of its functions and of its characteristic as a destination of trips, in order to emphasise that functions and traffic are inseparable. Some functions exist as a consequence of people's desire and ability to communicate with each other, sometimes for the purpose of trading. When these communications involve two people meeting face to face, or the collection or delivery of goods, a trip arises. Any consideration of urban problems must take account of the facts that changes in land-use, be they of kind or intensity, will probably affect the pattern of traffic, while changes in the ease with which trips may be made may affect the kind or intensity of land-use.

Land-use patterns and traffic are two related, but different, manifestations not simply of the desire to communicate, but also in our western society (as we have just suggested) of the desire to trade; and trade implies both specialisation and profit. As the volume of trade grows, so the opportunity to specialise increases. As the number of people practising a certain specialism increases, so there is a tendency for them to group together, sometimes simply for social purposes, but sometimes in order collectively to attract more custom, to benefit from an ability to co-operate as neighbours, and at the same time to be able to compete with each other as members of a localised market. It is chiefly for this reason that large towns tend to have their centres subdivided into many specialist centres. An understanding of decay in urban centres requires an examination of their trading function.

There have been many attempts to look at the ways in which this subdivision of the centre affects, and is affected by, such matters as rents, land values and redevelopment. Alfred Marshall used a similar approach when he wrote, towards the end of the nineteenth century, of the way in which 'shops which deal in expensive and choice objects tend to congregate together; and those which supply ordinary domestic needs do not'.[13] His very next sentence reads, 'Every cheapening of the means of communication, every new facility for the free interchange of ideas between distant places alters the action of the forces which tend to localize industries.' Then he moves to consider international freights and urban–rural flows. Communications within a town has no mention.

There is a slightly fuller account of Marshall's views in Appendix 5. The essential point is that he considered the nature and density of development of a site depended upon the marginal costs of additional development and the marginal returns derivable from its occupation. The latter would be influenced by its convenience or advantages to a potential user when compared with those of other sites, in different locations. These advantages could be affected by changes in transport.

It is, perhaps, not surprising that Marshall, an economist, should adopt an economic explanation of location. But this should not allow us to write it down simply to prejudice. Anybody using urban land has to weigh the value of the services he derives from it against the cost incurred through using it. This is the critical moment in reaching a decision about whether or not to occupy some land, and how to use it. It can be expressed as an economic decision, even though some of the services or costs may be described as social, aesthetic or something else. Other approaches to this problem may be found in the works mentioned in Appendix 5. We have cited Marshall's because our own is in some respects very similar to it. Before developing this, however, it will be useful for us to comment briefly on two much more recent theories. Each is concerned with land values and the location of different land-uses. Each is a simplification, attempting to produce a result broadly compatible with reality, but based on only a small number of decision criteria, and on assumptions that appear to simplify in the sense that they allow us to concentrate on the important or fundamental.

One of these has been put forward by William Alonso,[14] who begins with the usual assumption of a city on a featureless plain, with transport possible in all directions.

> All employment and goods and services are available only at the centre of the city. Land is bought and sold by free contract, without any institutional restraints and without having its character fixed by any structures existing upon the ground. Municipal services and tax rates are uniform throughout the city. The individual knows the price of the land at every location, and, from his point of view, this is a given fact, not affected by his decisions.

Here is an admittedly artificial city, in which many of the forces determining land values are assumed away. Nevertheless it enables us to make some interesting excursions into analysis.

Alonso argues that an individual will be able to spend his income between land costs, commuting costs and all other expenditures. He assumes that commuting costs increase with distance, and that land prices fall as one proceeds outwards from the centre of the town. For any individual the problem may be reduced to that of finding a place where he can live so that he gets as much total satisfaction as he can from his expenditures. Some of this arises from the amount of land that he occupies; some comes from the goods that he buys. From the total of these he has to subtract the dissatisfaction of commuting. Travel not only costs money, but it is, for him, a nuisance. He undertakes it only because by doing so he can live where land is cheaper, and so be able either to occupy more land or to buy more of other goods, or to do both. Alonso shows that the individual will settle only where the savings derived from cheaper land exceed the increased commuting costs.

When Alonso turns from the individual to the market he faces difficulties arising from the interrelationships of location, land price and commuting costs. To resolve them he considers first an urban firm whose profits depend on the volume of business, operating costs and land costs. He supposes that the volume of business depends on the size of the site and its distance from the centre. It is an assumption that implies that a business can be located non-centrally, and seems to contradict the initial assumption that all employment and goods and services are available only at the centre. The next assumption is that operating costs depend on site-area, distance from the centre and the volume of business, while land costs depend simply on area and distance. If the businessman attempts to maximise his profits, then it becomes possible for us to define his behaviour. In particular there will be a relationship between land rents and distance which is such that it just balances the other influences of distance on profit. It summarises the rents a firm would offer at each location and just be able to achieve a constant level of profits independent of the location.

For the individual who has no trading profit, there is a similar relationship, in which profit is replaced by satisfaction. For the agricultural land-user there is yet another relationship, depending on crop yields and prices.

Assuming the existence of three competing types of land-users, Alonso now sets them to bid against each other. The special complication is that they do so in a market in which 'there are two goods (land and distance) but only one transaction and one price (that of land)'. With a few further simplifying assumptions he reaches a solution in terms of game theory. A last chapter and a series of appendices brings back an air of realism as some of the assumptions are discussed and policies advocated. The fundamental contradiction between the two assumptions that all employment is available only at the centre of the town, but that urban firms may be located anywhere remains.

A different approach is that of Lowdon Wingo, Jr,[15] who likewise takes a simplified city, but treats transport differently, and divides the population into groups with different incomes and tastes. In his treatment of transport he considers both monetary and time costs. The former depends on distance and terminal congestion. Travelling time is priced according to the individual's marginal valuation of leisure, and then added to the direct monetary cost.

Unlike Alonso, who specifies that the preferences for land and accessibility are interrelated, Wingo assumes that the individual will spend the same total amount on land rent plus commuting, wherever he may reside. This amount is equal to the commuting costs incurred by somebody living so far out that land is rent-free. If the price of such land were to increase, the total amount spent by everybody on land plus commuting would increase, unless (of course) transport costs were to fall. Wingo stipulates that an individual would prefer more land to less, but that the higher the price the less of it he buys. These assumptions allow him to determine the amount of land bought by an individual and the price at which it is bought. The equilibrium market situations depend, of course, on the assumptions about group differences.

The understanding of a complex set of interactions often arises with the identification of a simple underlying mechanism, and it is in this sense that the theories we have just summarised were put forward by their authors. It is very easy to criticise the simple for not being complicated, just as it is easy to recognise complexity and to be defeated by it. In identifying some of the basic forces that are at work in the determination of land-use and land values, and in suggesting ways of analysing their effects, these authors have contributed a great deal to our understanding of urban change.

Operating beside these basic forces are others, which may sometimes exceed them in strength, and which always distort the pattern a clash of simple motives of profit maximisation by different potential users might suggest. There are, too, the constraints imposed by geography, history and institutions. The more one considers these, the more one must realise that the removal of awkward aspects of a problem in order to maintain mathematical tractability can be justified only if these aspects are not fundamental. It is our belief that some neglected factors, such as the surrender dates of leases, the intrusion of planned zoning of land-use and densities, and the two-way reaction between land-use and transport are fundamental. We must also keep in mind the market for tenancies, as opposed to the market for landownership, and speculation, which is an important real factor.

As a result of our study of Lower Deansgate we have evolved a set of comments on urban change, which we feel inclined to include in our theory. There is nothing novel about them, but we feel that a theory that ignores any of them has, at most, a very limited use. We also feel that a statement of them may, in itself, add something to our understanding of urban interdependencies.

When a firm or an individual has contracted to take up a lease for a given period, then normally that land-user does not re-enter the market for the same purpose until the lease has expired. (If the scale of his business alters, then he may have the new purpose of accommodating business on a new scale.) Similarly, the building or site that has been leased is usually removed from the market, in the sense that its owner is unable to dispose of its occupation until the lease has expired, unless he is willing to pay the lessee such compensation as he may require. On the other hand, some leases are not let immediately, some are short-term, while some sites and buildings may be sold freehold.

These considerations emphasise that at any moment of time the number of properties in fact available to a person seeking accommodation is only a small fraction of the total number of properties in the area. Since, in a given town, different areas tend to specialise in different functions, and even those devoted to the same land-use may be developed at different densities and standards, the effective choice before a prospective occupier may be very limited.

They also emphasise that the land-use pattern of a town results from a continuous sequence of decisions, taken at different moments over its whole life. The pattern that exists at any given moment is almost certain to be different from that which would exist if all the users of land were to be given costless simultaneous opportunities to change their locations. An adequate model of a town must start with some pattern that has a certain amount of resistance to change built into it, and the opportunities to change must descend upon land-users at different times.

When a building or site is let on a new lease, the rent is obviously related to the market value, but it need not be a simple relationship. The market value will affect the land-use. It will also reflect the demands for ownership arising from both private and public sectors, which we must now briefly consider in turn.

The demand for private ownership (as opposed to occupation) depends on many factors, including expectations of rental income during a leasing period, on the market value of the property at the expiration of the lease and on the costs of ownership and related development. None of these is determined in any simple way.

The expectations of rental income will depend on the expected demand for occupation of that site, reflecting the expected earnings the site may generate, on the availability of other sites and on other factors. In practice they may be based on knowledge of rents being received for neighbouring sites or for similar developments in other localities. Often they will be wrong.

The current expectations of future market value will necessarily be vague. This vagueness, allowing for the formation of different conclusions by different people in possession of the same facts, is an essential feature of reality, and should be included in our theory. If we assume that all neighbouring developments, policies and so on affecting the value of the land do so through affecting the rental income that can be derived from the land, then we can look upon the current expectations of future market value as expectations of future expectations of rent (plus future expectations of future future expectations . . . etc.). Even if land is purchased outright for the construction of a public highway, so that the owner is paid a lump sum, then this amount of money can be looked upon as a capitalisation of a perpetual income stream.

Costs of related development will depend upon demolition and construction costs, and on interest rates, which represent an opportunity cost of the development. Under this heading we must also consider the impact on demand for ownership of desires to remain liquid, for one of the costs of ownership is the loss of liquidity.

Different private persons and firms will behave in different ways, but all of them will be motivated by expectations rather than by certainties, and these expectations will in most cases take account of the factors we have just mentioned. But a great deal of the demand for ownership is public demand. It is here, strangely enough, that often the greatest uncertainty lies, and in assessing the probable future value of his land the private owner is often unable to take account of it. Costs of ownership and development affect it and a knowledge of these can sometimes help one to predict the course of public acquisition of land: but much uncertainty remains. Sometimes it is needless uncertainty.

It may be argued that any theory attempting to add factors such as these to the principles of marginalism and maximisation, as illustrated by the work of Alonso and Wingo, will be exceedingly complicated. This is so, but the complications are not unmanageable. At the heart of our theory must lie the demand for the private occupation of somebody else's land. Affected by many factors, including the expected income made possible by that occupation, it will help to determine the rental income and market value in the sense which we have just described. The different incomes and values arising from different uses and intensities will help to determine the development.

Before explaining how these matters can be examined in some detail, we must bring into our theory the difficult matter of traffic, and indicate how this approach to a study of towns can help us to understand decay.

It is perfectly clear from the Lower Deansgate study that parking problems and difficulties of collection and delivery may make an area so unattractive to an occupier that he leaves, unless there are overwhelming compensatory advantages in remaining or alternative communication or facilities supplied. In such a case, downward rental obsolescence is quite likely to set in. Even when there are no such problems, difficulties of access, because of congestion on the route, may have a similar result. For these reasons, accessibility and stopping or parking facilities may affect the value of a property, especially for certain uses, which may be very sensitive to these matters. Consequently they may affect land-use, and a change in land-use will affect traffic desires. There are clear regions in some of our towns of central areas that are declining, and seem to be doing so for reasons such as these.

It is, of course, true that the sheer volume of traffic causes environmental decay and functional inefficiencies. In some areas, especially where rebuilding is easy, it is possible to plan in a way that reduces, or even removes, both this aspect of the problem and the one we have just stressed. Unfortunately there is far too often an attempt to solve the problem simply by prohibiting stopping. Recently one of us heard from a director of a large company that has about 800 vans going around our towns, leaving clean towels for use in an automatic machine and collecting dirty ones. Their operations are hindered by 'no waiting' signs, which make it almost impossible for them to work in normal hours without breaking the law. To work outside those hours would involve considerable extra cost. Even the postman who stops his van to deliver a parcel may be fined. Traffic management seems so concerned with keeping the traffic moving that it does not allow it to stop. For some purposes the point at which a vehicle stops has to be the end of its trip. If stopping is prohibited, the trip becomes impossible, and functional obsolescence becomes nearer. On the other hand, the building and its surroundings may become more attractive to a new user.

In London the siting of the G.P.O. Tower in an area that has long been a traditional centre for a tightly knit community of small tailors, working largely for West End stores, has affected the trade. Here was an area occupied by rather seedy buildings, which were perfectly adequate from the viewpoint of their occupiers, who were sometimes their owners. Some were demolished in order to make room for the Tower. Now that the Tower exists there is a large tourist interest in the area. Higher rents can be obtained from souvenir shops and cafés. As short-term leases expire, tailors are asked for higher rents, and often they cannot afford them. They move to other places, in a way that disrupts this trading community and leads to a decline in its efficiency.

In Birmingham a similar disruption of a trading community was considered to be undesirable, and an attempt was made to prevent it. The traditional area of the jewellery trade was to be demolished, by a public decision, and the jewellers were offered alternative accommodation, as a community. The offer was unwelcome, because the new premises were substantially larger than most of the jewellers needed, and the rents were about three times as high as their previous rents.

These illustrations should not be interpreted as criticisms of the main aims of the policies mentioned. Possibly the location chosen for the G.P.O. Tower was in many ways better than any other. Possibly it is in the wider interests of the community to redevelop the area occupied by the jewellers in Birmingham. Our aim is simply to point to some of the complications that may grow out of our decisions, and to urge that there is need to study these. Urban decay is not to be studied simply as a symptom. One has to examine the causes of it, and these may be partly in our planning decisions, which may unexpectedly have either localised or generalised decay as one of their consequences. In an attempt to study matters such as these, there has recently been a move towards the construction of simulation models. To conclude this chapter we shall briefly indicate some of the main features of a model now being built in the Centre for Urban and Regional Research at Manchester University.

Let us begin by considering a model that could be built for a specified town if the necessary research resources were available. Suppose that the town is divided into a number of zones. The principles of division should be considered very carefully, although to do so now would be out of place. Some comments on the matter appear in Appendix 6. For our present purpose we shall suppose that the division has been accomplished. It is, in principle, possible to describe each zone in quantitative and attributive terms. Some of these relate to the zone itself, while others relate to some form of traffic or interaction between the zone and another zone. Here we use the word 'traffic' to include any flow of people, goods, services, ideas or materials. Atmospheric pollution blown from one zone to another is, in this sense, a form of traffic. So is a telephone call.

We may conveniently list some of the zonal characteristics that may be measured, simply to illustrate our ideas:

Area	Rents by building type
Perimeter	Numbers of empty properties
Largest diameter	Condition of buildings
Shortest diameter	Termination dates of leases
Population, by age and sex	Times taken to traverse zone in
Jobs, by type	different directions at various
Land-uses	times of day by various means
Development densities	Environmental standards
Age-structure of buildings	Social characteristics

Much of the information required under these headings does exist in one place or another. Other data could be obtained from surveys. The inter-zonal traffics of different kinds would be listed as flows across the zonal boundaries at different times of day. We may suppose that all of this information has been gathered for a period which, in terms of the rate of urban change, would be quite short. It could well be several months. We shall refer to it as 'a moment'.

At the analytical level, the first step is to formulate a set of behavioural hypotheses, involving some of the characteristics and traffics that we can measure. Examples of such hypotheses might be:

1. If parking is prohibited at any point within x yards of a chemist's shop and there is another chemist's shop within y yards without these restrictions, then within two months the first shop will lose z per cent of its trade.

2. Developers form their rental expectations by combining an extrapolation of recent trends in the zone concerned with an assessment of the 'correct' relationship with rents in other zones.

3. Once a developer has advertised some new offices at a specified rent, he will wait at least x months before accepting a lower rent.

4. The attractiveness of a particular location to a baker seeking a new retail outlet will depend upon the volume of pedestrian traffic, its nearness to a bus-stop, and the presence or absence of a similar shop.

5. Roads along which there is heavy traffic see a greater rate of turnover of occupants of premises than do other roads.

6. If a strong-knit community is moved from a slum area to a

block of flats, the frequency of personal contact within the community is reduced.

These are simply examples of hypotheses of the kind that we have in mind. Some, like the first, are capable of being set out in precise mathematical terms. Using the notation of that hypothesis we could write

$$z = \alpha + \beta x + \gamma y + \delta$$

where α, β and γ would have to be determined. The last term absorbs all other factors, supposed to be randomly distributed. There are standard statistical techniques for testing the validity of such a hypothesis, and for measuring β and γ. Other hypotheses, such as the last, are stated in a way that implies testing of a 'true or false' kind, without invoking the question 'how much'. It may, nevertheless, be possible to state our assumptions with various degrees of precision.

This approach can help us in two ways. As each hypothesis is tested and refuted or accepted, we add to our knowledge of the forces that govern urban decay.

If, however, these hypotheses are properly integrated and sufficiently numerous, it may be possible for us to take a description of a town, according to the characteristics of its many zones and the inter-zonal traffic, at a given moment, and then to use our tested hypotheses to generate a description for a later moment. In this way we could simulate the changing town affected by 'natural' forces or those imparted by planned policy.

It may immediately be pointed out that such an automatic and mechanical approach would fail to take account of those many unpredictable factors that have a real influence on urban development. This need not be a valid objection. It is perfectly possible to formulate a model in which every single decision has a 'rational' component and an 'irrational' one. Adequate field-work would enable us to identify the areas of decision on which chance plays the greatest part.

For us to see the use of such a model, we must dwell on this point a little longer. Nobody could hope ever to predict with complete accuracy the detailed statistical description of a town in even five years' time. It is, however, quite reasonable to assert that, with adequate work along the lines just described, we should be able to produce a useful range of predictions. By feeding in a large number of different sets of 'chance events', each supplementing a 'rational part of the process of urban change, we could obtain a large number of predictions, each compatible with our initial description of the town and our tested hypotheses.

Now let us suppose that we know what one of the 'chance events' is going to be. It may be the erection of a school, the closure of a railway station, the abolition of car-parking or some other matter over which we have some control. In such a case we could run the model for another set of predictions, keeping all other chance events exactly the same as before.

The result will be two sets of predictions. In each pair, one assumes the existence of a school (or whatever it may be), while the other assumes its non-existence. Comparison of the two sets should enable us to see fairly clearly both the possible and the probable consequences on any aspect of the town in which we are interested of the policy under consideration.

This is a possibility of great importance. To keep to our first example, the siting of a school will, for many reasons, alter the attractiveness for residential purposes of a large area. The concentrated pedestrian, cycle and other vehicular trips to and from the school will create traffic interference, which may be felt over a wide area. What is the total addition to the time taken to travel by car into a town centre due to the siting of a single school on one side of the road rather than on the other? What is the impact on shopkeepers of spending by the school-children? How does this affect rents and expenditure on maintenance? How different would it have been if the school had been elsewhere?

These are but a few of the questions to which we have only the vaguest answers. Probably a vague answer is often adequate, but every town has its history of planning decisions with unexpected consequences and of urban changes (including the surrender of tenancies and the onset of decay) that are still unexplained. A model of the kind we have just described can help us to understand.

The remaining question is whether such a model may require resources beyond our means. Part of the answer to this must be that it may very well be worth devoting a great deal of resources to this kind of work, for ill-informed decisions often have costly consequences. Unfortunately, public expenditure on research has to be voted, while the cost of adverse consequences is often disguised and rarely attributable with conviction to public action.

A resource-saving device not to be despised is the construction of a purely artificial model. One begins with a statistical description of an artificial town and assumes that certain hypotheses are valid. The model is then put in motion to evolve a set of predictions. Several courses are then open to one. The consequences in the artificial town of a public policy or planning decision may be examined. If they are a little unexpected, it may be useful to inquire whether this could be so in a real town. Another possibility is experimentation with alternative assumptions, which may help us to identify areas of behaviour in which a precise understanding seems to be more important than in others. It may be, for example, that the future pattern of a town depends very much on how developers assess rents, but very little on how they estimate costs. In such a case the research worker with limited resources will have some guidance on which to base his priorities.

In Manchester we are compromising between these approaches by building an artificial model, but by feeding into it such data and tested hypotheses as our resources will allow us to obtain for a real town. A somewhat fuller account of our ideas is given in Appendix 7, which also suggests a way in which it may become possible for us to produce one single general model, capable of being a model of any specific town when the necessary data are fed into it.

This has not been a complete account of the forces of urban change, or even a balanced account. Our aim has been to show how the study of a town as a whole can lead to a better understanding of the consequences of our actions. Decay is part of urban change. If it is to be understood, the town has to be studied as a whole, both qualitatively and quantitatively. Urban measurement and the testing of hypotheses about urban change are still on an inadequate scale.[16]

CHAPTER 6

A Policy towards Decay

The last chapter advocated an elaborate research programme into urban change. But action cannot always wait for complete understanding. We need a policy that will allow maximum use of the knowledge we have already obtained, yet have sufficient flexibility for knowledge acquired later to be used.

A policy concerning decay must have two parts. One should be concerned with the decay that already exists. The other should be concerned with the problem of how to plan, design, build and legislate, so that in future decay will be less of a problem than it is now, and so that we not only control it, but even, perhaps, turn it to advantage.

We may begin by asking three related questions. How much decay is there now? How rapidly is the need for new building going to grow? How quickly is the demand for urban land going to increase? When we have answered these questions we will have some idea of the magnitude of the problem for which we must have a policy.

At a naïve level one may take the period of, say, seventy-five years as the useful life of a building. It exceeds the longest period over which even local authorities can borrow. If one does this, then one can infer that since the 1890s contained a large building boom, with the annual rate of house-building doubling between 1890 and 1899, then a considerable eruption lies before us. Alternatively, if we take the lifetime at a hundred years, then the preceding upswing in house-building, which roughly doubled in volume between 1865 and 1876, is about to have its replacement echo.[1]

The fact that this is a naïve approach must not blind us to the possibility of learning something from it. Clearly even a thousand identical houses built in adjacent streets in the same year may have different lifetimes. Different owners and occupiers may spend money on them at different rates and in different ways, and in the normal course of events one may expect to find fairly substantial differences in their condition. Houses of different kinds built in different places, with all the implied differences of weather and atmospheric pollution, may be even more different in their resistance to the forces of time. A comparison of working-class terraces in Northern towns with those in the South tends to add subjective confirmation to this idea. Yet one must also note the tendency of similarly aged and built houses to be in roughly the same condition if they are reasonably near to each other.

There are good reasons for this. Houses of a similar kind in a given district are market substitutes for each other. They are subject to almost identical social and economic forces. Likely to be occupied by people of similar incomes and tastes, or to be the property of similar (or identical) owners, they will be treated in much the same way. Rent control, which has existed to some degree for over half a century and has taken rateable value as the basis of its incidence, has provided another push towards uniformity of maintenance expenditure on similar properties. It is no accident that a description such as 'late Victorian villa in South Manchester', or 'mid-Victorian terraced cottage in Oldham' conjures up a fairly precise vision not only of design, but also of general outward appearance. It may be wrong in detail, but there is a good chance that it is right in general.

On the other hand, when sufficient funds have been available, it has often been possible to maintain, to adapt or to convert Victorian and Edwardian buildings so that they compare favourably with current standards. The carcass of the building has often proved to be more durable than the internal design or the equipment and fittings. This uneven obsolescence of the parts has to some extent contributed towards decay, but in other cases it has made possible a gradual piecemeal rehabilitation.

We shall return to the points we have just made when we consider methods of measurement based on field studies. Meanwhile, however, we may look at one or two calculations based on published statistics. Most of these come from population censuses and returns of rateable value.

There were in 1966 about 17,400,000 houses and flats in England and Wales. Of these between 10,000,000 and 11,000,000 were pre-war houses. If we assume that post-war houses will not require replacement during this century, but that during the next thirty-three years we aim at replacing three-quarters of our pre-war stock, then we arrive at an average annual replacement programme of about 230,000–250,000 houses. At the end of the century we would be left with about 2,500,000 houses aged more than seventy years. Presumably most of them would have been built between the wars. A programme that would leave no pre-war houses would require an average annual replacement figure of about 320,000 houses. These two programmes would imply total replacements by 1980 of 3,200,000 and 4,200,000 houses respectively.

These are figures worth keeping in mind, not because any sensible programme would take age as the sole criterion for demolition, but because they help us to see against a historical perspective the implication of programmes based on other criteria, such as those we now consider. There are many estimates of the extent of rehousing that is currently necessary, and the rate at which this will change in the next decade or so. Rather than embark upon a new set of calculations, we may comment on some of the estimates that have been made and move towards some plausible range within which the figure probably lies.

In its report *The North-West: a regional study*,[2] the Department of Economic Affairs suggests three rather rough guides to the extent of substandard housing. One is the number of dwellings (other than farm workers' dwellings) with a rateable value of £30 or less. It remarks that these dwellings can be regarded, 'whatever the area, as representing a substandard category of accommodation. Dwellings within this category are generally old, small and of poor quality and can certainly be regarded as potential, if not actual, slums.'

It turns out that 18·5 per cent in 1965 of the total housing stock of England and Wales fell into this category. This amounts to almost 2,600,000 dwellings. One-fifth of them are in the North-West, whereas many as a quarter of all dwellings are in this substandard category. In Glamorgan, Durham and the West Riding of Yorkshire the percentages are as high as 26·6, 30·2 and 38·2. A second guide to the situation is provided by the percentage of dwellings without fixed baths in 1961. For England and Wales this comes to 22·0, while for the North-West it is 24·9. A third indicator is one that give us an upper boundary for the numbers of houses older than a certain age. In 1861 the total number of dwellings enumerated in England and Wales was 27 per cent of the number enumerated in 1961. Some of these will have since been demolished, as will some that have been built more recently. It is likely that of the houses standing in 1961 rather less than a quarter had been built before 1861. When we take a more recent date, we find that in 1881 the number enumerated was 36 per cent of the 1961 number. We may infer that probably rather less than a third of all existing houses were built before 1881. Actually the years between 1861 and 1881 saw a great upswing in house-building, especially between 1870 and 1876, followed by a great collapse. While perhaps something like one house in twelve or thirteen now standing was built in these twenty years, a third of these were erected in the short space of five years, between 1874 and 1878.

Translated into round numbers, these pointers suggest that out of the 14,000,000 houses enumerated in England and Wales in 1961 some 2,600,000 were substandard on the rateable-value test. If we apply the bath test, then the number falling below standard is 3,000,000. The number of houses built before 1861 and still standing a hundred years later was probably less than 3,500,000, while the number that will probably reach their centenary (if they are not first demolished) between 1961 and 1981 is something like 1,200,000.

It is, of course, just not true to say that all houses without baths need demolishing. Nor is it true that all houses older than a certain age are ripe for demolition. On the other hand, the vast majority of the industrial cottages built before 1880 were of standards now considered to be deplorably low, even if they were often better than those of the agricultural cottages that formerly housed their tenants. Adaptations have sometimes taken place, and many of these houses have been saved from becoming miserable hovels.

Just as some houses that are now eighty years old will still be in good condition in twenty years' time, so others are already decayed. If we are attempting to predict the number of houses that will need replacement in the next twenty years, then we need information about present conditions, rate of depreciation, maintenance expenditures, life of materials and a host of other factors. We do not have these in sufficient detail. Even if we did, our predictions would have wide margins of possible error attached to them. It seems that we might as well look at the indicators we have mentioned and assert that in 1961 there were between 2,600,000 and 3,500,000 houses in need of renewal, and that by 1981 about another 1,000,000 will have been added to these. It is, however, important to keep in mind that renewal does not necessarily mean complete demolition and replacement.

We may check these magnitudes by using a most useful survey of housing conditions in the Town and Country Planning Association Survey, *Housing in Britain*, published in 1964. Pointing out that the number of substandard dwellings was bound to depend on the standards adopted, the compilers of this survey looked at the problem from several viewpoints. They concluded that 'if all the houses in England and Wales were now assessed on the highest standard used by local authorities in the 1954/55 survey, it is likely that at least one million of them would be found unfit or suitable for action under the Housing Act of 1957' (op. cit. p.49).

At various times the Government has introduced legislation for improvement grants. They have been concerned with ensuring that houses have certain minimum standards of facilities, such as hot water, a food store, and so on. In 1959 the House Purchase and Housing Act made certain provisions that would operate for houses not unfit according to the standards of the 1957 Act, and which had an expected lifetime of at least fifteen years. The Social Survey estimated in mid-1960 that 1,950,000 households in England and Wales lived in dwellings that were thus ineligible for assistance under the Act. A further 4,300,000 lived in houses with an estimated life of at least fifteen years, but lacking one or more of the following: a hot-water supply, a wash basin, a fixed bath (or a shower in bathroom), a water closet in or attached to the dwellings.

Housing in Britain also refers to the Twelve Point Standard laid down by the Housing (Financial Provisions) Act, 1958. The authors suggest that there are perhaps about 2,750,000 accommodation units that are not now up to standard, but could be brought up to it. After looking at various other standards they produce an estimate of 'housing need' for England and Wales, which we print in Table 7.

It is clear that some of these estimates are very different from others. However, the difference is perhaps not as great as it looks, for the single figure of 4,310,000 households lacking at least one of the amenities listed in the table conceals a wide range of standards. Many of the dwellings concerned could be brought up to standard with comparatively little trouble or cost, while others are almost certainly in need of considerable alteration or even demolition. In some cases it may be necessary to combine adjacent dwellings into a single dwelling if the minimum amenities are to be provided. Con-

TABLE 7. THE *Housing in Britain* ESTIMATE OF HOUSING NEED IN
ENGLAND AND WALES

Dwellings needed by households who:
  lived in houses that are, or ought to have been,
    declared unfit: 1,000,000
  lived in houses with a life of less than 15 years in
    mid-1960:   950,000
  did not have a bath, wash basin, hot-water supply
    or water closet, and lived in houses other than
    those listed above: 4,310,000
  lived in caravans, etc.   50,000
                                                          ―――――――――
                                                          6,310,000
                                                          ―――――――――

SOURCE: *Housing in Britain*, Table 6.2.

sideration of the estimates just cited suggests that in broad figures
the situation may be something like the following:

Number of houses needing demolition and
  replacement by 1975 if minimum standards
  are to be maintained: 2,000,000

Number of houses needing additional amenities
  of adaptation or demolition and replacement
  (in addition to above) at present: 4,000,000

This is very similar to the previous table, but the wording is more
explicit.

The Housing White Paper published in November 1965 (Cmnd
2838) put existing replacement needs at about 1,000,000 to replace
unfit houses already identified as slums and 'up to two million more
to replace old houses not yet slums but not worth improving'. It also
specified replacements of about 30,000 per annum to replace the
loss caused by demolition, road widening and other forms of redevelopment.

After this chapter had been completed, the Government published
Old Houses into New Homes, which contains the results of a sample
survey conducted early in 1967. According to this 'there are probably
1·8 million unfit dwellings in England and Wales'. In addition, 'about
4·5 million dwellings which are not unfit require either £125 or more
spent on repairs, or lack one or more basic amenities or both'.

These sample estimates accord closely with the estimates reached above, and consequently we have left the remainder of this chapter untouched.

In recent years conversions and improvements under the Housing Acts have been proceeding at the rate of about 45,000 per annum, while demolitions under the same Act have averaged about 65,000 per annum. Clearly the estimates we have just summarised imply that a considerable acceleration in their programme is necessary. On the other hand, there have been uncounted conversions and demolitions that have not been under the powers of the Acts concerned.

The proportion of the 4,000,000 houses at present needing alteration or demolition and which will in fact have enough money spent on them to preserve them beyond 1980 is unknown. The Government can offer incentives of various kinds, but our knowledge of the subject is so abysmally undocumented that we do not even know whether maintenance and adaptation are, from the national point of view, the best use of resources. It is a question to which we shall return.

This rough estimate of the numbers of houses needing replacement or substantial attention gives us some measure of the task we face: but it tells us nothing about the conditions of our shops, offices and other buildings. On the other hand, these other premises have been spared the adverse effects of rent control and security of tenure, and both maintenance and redevelopment have been motivated more noticeably by market forces and public policy. Whether shops and offices decay or change in other ways is a matter of great importance: but quantitatively the volume of decay is slight when compared with residential decay.

We must now consider the housing needs that will arise from population growth and other changes. Forecasts of population can always be challenged, but we are prepared to accept the suggestion that in the year 2001 the population of England and Wales is likely to be something like the 66 million forecast by the Registrar-General, compared with 46 million in 1961. This increase of about 44 per cent over a period of forty years is not unprecedented. Between 1821 and 1861, for example, the population increased at a much faster rate than this, as it also did between 1861 and 1901. But between 1901 and 1941 the increase—over forty years—was only 9 million people, representing an increase of under 30 per cent. In terms of percentages our population is expected to increase at a faster rate than it has so far done in this century. In terms of absolute numbers we are expecting an addition far exceeding any that a period of forty years has previously witnessed.

This increase of population will not be at a constant rate, if only because of the existing age-structure of our population, which now has an abnormally high proportion of people aged around twenty due to the post-war peak in births. This is a factor that will shortly affect the rate of household formation. If one applies age-specific marriage rates to the existing population, one finds that the annual number of marriages is likely to rise slightly until about 1970 and then to decline quite sharply before a second upswing appears in the late seventies. It happens that there was also a substantial and sharp change in our birth rate at the turn of the century, and this will shortly produce a peak in the numbers of elderly people who will be dying or surrendering their homes. This coincidence of a trough in marriages with a peak in the rate of surrender of houses is bound to have a profound impact on the demand for new houses. We must look at it in more detail.

Marriages and deaths are not the only components of net household formation, even though they are the more important ones; and household formation is not the only component in the demand for houses. Two factors are often mentioned as reasons for asserting that the demand for new houses will continue to grow. They are household-fission and rising incomes.

The household-fission argument states that for a variety of reasons we can expect more and more young single people to establish homes of their own. This will be especially true if incomes rise rapidly, and in this case we can also expect more and more people to acquire second houses, as week-end and holiday retreats. Continental and American experience is used as evidence to support these arguments.

It would be foolish to close our eyes to these possibilities, even though one might argue that different countries have different traditions and different land availabilities, and that consequently what happens in some countries may be little guide to what may happen in others. What matters for the present argument (which is centred around the assertion that demand for additional houses will fall in the early and middle seventies) is whether these two forces are likely to be strong enough to offset the effects of a decline of about 25 per cent in the rate of net household formation estimated by conventional 'headship' calculations that do not take these factors into account.

We may first consider household-fission. Here there are two essential points, which may be illustrated by a hypothetical example. Suppose that every year 1000 people reach the age of seventeen and then set up households of their own. Let all of these people marry (each other) at the age of twenty. The 1000 people setting up households will require 1000 houses (or flats). When they marry, the number of households falls, and the net reduction in households due to marriages is 500 per annum. The net increase in household formation is thus 500 per annum.

Now suppose that, instead of setting up their own one-person households at the age of seventeen, they all live at home until the age of twenty, when they get married. The net increase in households is, once again, 500 per annum.

Finally, let us suppose that there is a changing pattern of existence, with an increasing proportion of people setting up home before they are twenty. The detailed assumptions and their consequences may be read from Table 8. Briefly, we assume that initially nobody sets up home before he gets married, but that things gradually change, and within thirteen years everybody sets up a single-person household at the age of seventeen.

The result is a sharp rise in household formation, reaching a peak in five years, and then a slow decline to its original level by the sixteenth year.

This is, of course, a very artificial example. The sharp rise occurs because we assume a very rapidly changing social habit. In the first year there are no single households. In the third year 30 per cent of single people are in households of their own. If we had let changes occur only a quarter as fast, so that in the third year there would have been 75 single households and in the fourth year 150, and so on, then the net increase in household formation would have risen from 500 in the first year to 600 in the fourth year and 625 in the fifth year. But even this increase of 25 per cent in the rate of net household formation over a period of five years would require a change over that quinquennium from no single-person households to a situation in which 22·5 per cent of our single-persons aged seventeen to nineteen would be living alone. It is quite possible that one day this will be so. But what matters is whether the change will

TABLE 8. EXAMPLES OF EFFECTS OF HOUSEHOLD-FISSION

(1)	(2)	(3)	(4)	(5)	(6)	(7)	(8)	(9)	(10)
	Number of people who set up single-person households at age			Total single-person households formed	Number of single-person households ceasing due to marriage at age 20 of persons who set up households			Number of two-person households set up by marriage at age 20	Net increase in number of households $= (9)+(5) -((6)+(8)+(7)+(8)$
Year	17	18	19		1	2	3		
					years earlier				
1	0	0	0	0	0	0		500	500
2	0	0	100	100	0	0		500	600
3	0	100	200	300	100	0		500	700
4	100	200	300	600	200			500	900
5	200	300	400	900	300	100		500	1000
6	300	400	300	1000	400	200		500	900
7	400	400	200	1000	300	300	100	500	800
8	500	400	100	1000	200	400	200	500	700
9	600	400	0	1000	100	400	300	500	700
10	700	300	0	1000	0	400	400	500	700
11	800	200	0	1000	0	400	500	500	600
12	900	100	0	1000	0	300	600	500	600
13	1000	0		1000	0	200	700	500	600
14	1000			1000	0	100	800	500	600
15	1000			1000	0		900	500	600
16	1000			1000	0		1000	500	500
17	1000			1000	0		1000	500	500

occur at something approaching this rate. The slower the change the less noticeable the effect will be. It does not seem likely that the period between now and the early seventies will see a very rapid change in social habits.

The second point may be made more briefly. The single-person households that teenagers may establish will only rarely have the finance for a house. The demand is much more likely to be for bed-sitters and similar accommodation. There is probably more of this available than is apparent from our statistics, and a substantial part of the demand could well be met through an increase in the practice of sub-letting. Household-fission does not necessarily mean demand for houses.

The extent to which our demands may change in response to income changes is unknown. The necessary research into income-elasticities of demand in this country has not been done. It is important that this and other research into household formation and housing demand should be given high priority. Meanwhile, although it is unlikely that rising incomes will lead to a substantially increased demand in the next few years, we must keep this possibility in mind. We also need to do more research into the sizes and kinds of houses that people want and for which they are prepared to pay.

There are two major components in the total demand for house-building. One is net household formation. The other is rehousing. There is also a plea from many quarters for smooth economic growth, and, in particular, the building industry asserts (correctly in our opinion) that it could be much more efficient if it could grow smoothly. This means that if there is a period when we expect net household formation to be low, then that is the time when it may be most efficient for us to concentrate on rehousing.

Thus we have a period of perhaps two or three years before we find ourselves presented with a golden opportunity. We have calculated that, if we increase our production by 8000 or 9000 houses per annum every year until 1980, we will not only have a smoothly growing and efficient industry, but we will also cope quite generously with the demands for new housing and rehousing. But to start building 500,000 houses per annum in the near future would certainly lead to over-supply and to a sharp fall in activity of a kind that would have unfortunate circumstances throughout the economy.

Between 1960 and 1963 the annual number of houses completed for private owners in Great Britain varied between 168,000 and

177,000. But in 1964 it leaped to 218,000 and in the next year it was 214,000. Meanwhile in the public sector a similar phenomenon occurred. Between 1960 and 1963 the annual rate was between 118,000 and 130,000. Then, in 1964, came a leap to 156,000, and the next year to 168,000. From then on the two sectors have moved in different directions. Private housing declined to 205,000 in 1966, while public housing rose to 180,000. Early 1967 saw an increase as mortgage difficulties eased and builders rushed to commence activities before April, to avoid the payment of charges to the Land Commission. Perhaps this is the beginning of a lasting upswing, but it would be unwise to assume that it is so. Is it possible that the demand for houses for owner-occupation has passed its peak? It is a question we must ask, even if we cannot yet answer it.

As far as we can work it out, the current annual rate of net household formation is around 120,000. In other words, it is lower than the number of new houses built each year for private owners. It is less than a third of our total output of houses. With the public sector building something like 100,000 houses a year in excess of its demolition programme, the total number of houses now becoming available for new households is around 300,000 per annum. For every additional family there are now being supplied about two and a half houses.

There are, of course, marked regional differences. These crude calculations have also paid inadequate attention to standards and to the backlog of the dissatisfied. Nevertheless the point we have made is an important one. If building rates are expanded much above their present levels, then only a vast demolition programme, perhaps, indeed, of houses few of us would today condemn, will sustain them, unless there is a truly remarkable shift towards owner-ship of summer cottages and so forth. The full force of this argument will be seen in the early and middle seventies.

We now turn to the demands that will be made upon land. Appendix 8 outlines some calculations of the urban land requirements implied by the growth of population, with some acceptance of modern standards. It suggests that they may increase from 3·6 million acres for 1951 to 6·5 million acres by 2001. Of this about 28 per cent will be needed simply to provide extra space for the houses, offices, shops and schools that already exist, but crowded together in the substandard areas of some of our towns. Most of the increase will be at the expense of agricultural land.

Since the total supply of land is limited, its allocation between different uses is a problem of considerable importance. In a free-market economy the matter would be settled simply by the price mechanism, and since the urban uses can generate much greater incomes than agricultural uses, very little account would be taken of agricultural worth. The present green-belt policy and other planning policies restricting the areas in which land may be used for urban purposes are probably very beneficial in some ways; but, by concentrating demand in certain areas, they inevitably drive up the free-market price. Although it is disputed by others, the opinion of many economists is that the operation of the Land Commission is likely to do the same, even though some of the gain in value arising out of development will be passed back to the community.

As the demands upon agricultural land by urban uses increase, and are to some extent satisfied, so the opposition to further demands will grow. Prices are likely to rise further, when sales are effected, and there will be increased pressure by those who may be concerned about agriculture for urban development to take place on land that is less suitable for agriculture (but which may also be less good from the point of view of those who have to develop or to live in the town). Even if land were to be completely nationalised, and the price mechanism, as we know it, abolished, the opportunity-cost of re-allocating a piece of land from agricultural to urban use would have to be considered, and this would be bound to rise as the total claims of urban use increase. As our population grows and requires more feeding, the gains in agricultural yield brought about by intensive farming and fertilising improvements are likely to be to a large extent, if not completely, cancelled. The future of British agriculture is, of course, already made rather uncertain by our possible entry into the Common Market, and there are more distant global relationships that may yet bear heavily on the assumptions that are the foundations of our present agricultural policy. It may be that in some respects farming is, and must always remain, inefficient, and that a diminution in the effort we devote to growing our own food might eventually lead to a more efficient use of our total resources of land and labour. We do not know. What we have to remember is that any reallocation of land to a non-agricultural use is a process that can be reversed—in thirty, forty or a hundred years' time—only at great cost. It may well be that by some such date the worth to the community of agricultural land will be much greater than now, especially since our population is growing. Before we reduce its supply, we should consider more carefully than we do what it is that we are doing.

This is a problem of particular importance in certain areas. One can look at this at two levels. On the one hand is the purely local level, where there are competing demands for land by industry, agriculture, housing, recreation and other uses (all of which may grow with affluence and rising population). These may be particularly intense at certain places where there are scenic or other locational advantages, but in most cases these demands will reflect (with comparatively minor modifications due to site characteristics) the general levels of demands for these land-uses over a wider area. While all plots of land are individually unique, few are such that there is no tolerably acceptable substitute, and usually the most acceptable substitutes are fairly close at hand. It is, indeed, precisely for this reason that much of the difference in regional land value exists. At this second, regional, level the broader aspects of the problem not only are more easily analysed, but also are seen to be the more important. If, for example, there were a large exodus from the South-East, with a consequent diminution in the demands for all land-uses, prices of land in that region would fall generally.

The ways in which population growth will vary from region to region must be of some concern to us. Forecasts are difficult. We know that birth, marriage and death rates vary quite a bit from region to region. There is also migration. If we assume that each region grows at a rate proportional to its growth rate over 1951–61, but multiplied up to give a national total in 2001 agreeing with the Registrar-General's estimates, we get the picture shown in Table 9. We are not presenting these as forecasts, for there is no reason why present regional growth rates should continue. These are estimates that give us an idea of what will happen if they do. Much of the inequality in growth rates stems from migration, and from 1951 to 1961, at any rate, the Midlands and South and especially the South-East were the gainers. If they continue to be, then in very broad terms the above pattern may develop. In the first half of the fifties, when Great Britain suffered a net loss by migration of about 37,000 persons per annum (on average), Scotland, Wales and the North of England were all net losers, the South was a net gainer, as were the Midlands. Essentially this has remained the position

TABLE 9. PROBABLE POPULATION GROWTH, BY REGIONS, IN ENGLAND
AND WALES

Region	1961	Estimate for 2001
South-East	17·8	27·9
Midlands	8·4	12·7
North	14·0	18·6
South-West	3·1	4·7
Wales	2·6	3·3
England and Wales	45·9	66·4

ever since. Although the second half of the fifties saw Great Britain reverse its net migration loss, as immigrants averaged 46,000 persons more than emigrants every year, the regional effect was that the South and Midlands gained more than previously, whereas in the North every region was still a net loser. The Northern Planning Region (defined as the counties of England north of Yorkshire and Lancashire, with the addition of the North Riding of Yorkshire) lost rather less than previously, but otherwise the quinquennium was much the same as the previous one. The Midlands and the South were the net gainers not only of the 46,000 surplus of immigrants over emigrants, but also of 62,000 persons who drifted from the North, Scotland and Wales. Over the whole quinquennium the net gain to the Midlands and South, 540,000 persons, was four times as large as in the previous five years.

This consequence of immigration from overseas and the drift from the North was not unnoticed at the time. Equally in the public eye was the fact that in several of the areas that were losing population there was high unemployment. It was, indeed, largely as a result of calls for action to provide more, and more stable, employment in these areas that emphasis began once again to be placed on encouraging development in selected areas. Whether it was the best long-term interests of the country for these areas to grow or to decline is a question that was not faced squarely. They were selected because it was (and is) politically difficult to ignore the cries for action when men are out of work, or when women who wish to work find no suitable local opportunities. It may, nevertheless, be the

case that this political response to one aspect of the regional employment problem, coupled with the reaction to the problems of congestion that were becoming more and more apparent in the South, was
in fact a sound long-term move.

When the sixties began, an interesting change was appearing,
marking to a considerable extent the success of the regional policies.
Between 1961 and 1964 the Yorkshire and Humberside region,
which had lost about 10,000 persons in the previous decade, gained a
total of 3000. Migration from the North-West, which had averaged
12,000 per annum in the previous decade, ceased. Farther north,
but still in England, net emigration slightly fell, while Wales became
a net receiver of population. But the exodus from Scotland gathered
pace. Augmenting the net immigration from overseas of 75,000
persons per annum, it enabled the Midlands to grow even faster
than previously, the South-West to gain 24,000 per annum and the
South-East (despite some official discouragement and all the evils of
congestion) still to gain nearly 200,000 persons in three years. Yet
over the period when these changes were testifying, to some extent
at least, to the success of regional policies, a great deal of official
and other influential thinking was geared to the passive acceptance
of 'drift' or the perpetuation of existing patterns. In his book *London
2000* Peter Hall based his view of employment planning on the
'fundamental thesis that economic forces cannot be halted or
reversed' (p. 69), and thus 'it behoves us to accept wholeheartedly
this continued growth in London Region' (p. 67). He maintained
that 'planners are not free to manipulate the geography of employment' (p. 43). The theme was soon provided with official support.
In evolving a policy for the railways Dr Beeching focused attention
on the purely accounting criterion for deciding on the future of
branch lines. Those which, by remaining open but making a loss,
might help to prevent drift, or eventually to help growth were to be
closed except in cases of extreme hardship. In the case of railways,
public money was not to be spent in an attempt 'to manipulate the
geography of employment'. More recently, in explaining the decision
not to develop the port of Portbury, near Bristol, the Ministry of
Transport has pointed out that studies of our existing ports have
shown that those that are economically most viable are those that
have a fairly sizeable industrial hinterland within a certain radius,
and that because Bristol does not, at present, have such a hinterland,
the port should not be developed. Whether it may be in the interests

of the country to provide such a port, which would help to create its hinterland, has not been explicitly considered.

Examples of this kind abound. One can, of course, also instance cases where a more enlightened attitude has prevailed; but they are insufficient. There was a time when industrialists and governments looked at the national economy in terms of this thesis. The violent fluctuations of employment that were the outcome of the nine-teenth-century trade-cycle were inevitable, in their eyes, for they stemmed from those economic forces which, like Hall, they consider-ed to be irresistible and irreversible. Hall's fundamental thesis is one that today must be considered wrong. Although we have not yet reached the stage where we can iron out those fluctuations in the level of employment that so characterised the old trade-cycle, we have—as the whole of post-war economic history testifies—reached a stage in which both upswings and downswings in economic activity can be halted by government intervention; and the halt can be followed by a reversal. It may be true that individual economic forces cannot be halted or reversed, but they can certainly be countered by other economic forces which we are able to command (with a timelag and a degree of uncertainty), and in this way the resultant force, made up out of all the others, may have a new direction. We have done this in our purely economic planning. We can do it on a regional basis, and are, indeed, already doing it. The geography of employment depends to some extent on the geography of invest-ment. An industrialist wishing to build a new factory will take many matters into account, including relative prospects of profit that may arise in different locations. To some extent these will depend on labour availability and so forth. They will also depend on invest-ment costs (including investment grants), on taxation of profits or incomes (which may be varied regionally), on operating costs (which may be altered by public transport provisions) and on many other economic considerations, as well as on controls of various kinds. Many of these are matters we can manipulate, either in response to political pressures or as part of a definite long-term policy about the location of industrial and residential growth in this country. The Regional Employment Premium is one instance of the acceptance of this ideal even though it is based on the not necessarily correct conception that it is more important to even out unemployment percentages than to have a sound, forward-looking regional policy.

It may be argued that the geography of employment should not be manipulated in this way, or that, alternatively, the manipulation should not be done by 'planners'. Our own position may be summarised in a few contentions. We believe that towns have to be viewed not piece by piece, but as wholes. We believe that they must be viewed in their regional contexts, and that the regional economies and communities of which they are part must be taken in their national context. The social and economic interdependencies of the regions mean that development in one region will affect another. It also means that there may be some point in asking whether the country's interest, defined in some way or the other, is best served by encouraging faster growth in one region than in another, or by encouraging a different kind of development in the North than in the South. Is it, for example, in the interest of our leisure, or of our balance of payments, to develop heavy industry in Devon, which may create more and 'better' employment opportunities, but make it a less desirable place for retirement and holidays? Is it in the interests of the efficiency of our communications and the prosperity of those sectors of our economy with large transport costs to develop industry in areas at present underdeveloped, even at the cost of subsidised railways? May it be in our long-term interests to let some regions decline in industrial importance and to compensate those who lose their work and have to migrate?

These and similar questions have not been answered yet, but they will go on being asked until a satisfactory answer is forthcoming. Because of this we are to a large extent manipulating (sometimes by default or accident) the geography of employment, without knowing why or whether our various manipulations are consistent either with each other or with some unspecified long-term aims. We still have not faced up to the problem of specifying the kind of Britain that we want to see in the year 2001. A few dreams have been put forward, but none has paid sufficient regard to the questions of how they are to be attained, whether (with the same resources) one could attain something 'better', or whether the new Britain of the dream unnecessarily deprives still more distant generations of opportunities to shape their own future. In practice, decisions that are bound to have long and far-reaching consequences on land-use, regional development and the fabric of our towns are being reached on a basis of *ad hoc* expediency. The earlier decisions about the Third London Airport are an example.

The specification of Utopia will never lead to agreement, and rarely leads to action. One can, however, suggest that we may try to distribute our industry and population in a way that provides acceptable living standards, efficient use of our resources (including our geography) and opportunity for future generations to adapt what they inherit from us to suit their own needs with as little restriction as possible. To some extent the means of achieving these aims can be determined from answers to the kind of questions we have just posed. The use of budgetary and other economic measures for the encouragement of regional growth must not be forgotten. It would, however, be wrong to think that the existence of abundant work and high wages is the sole determinant of regional growth. There are some factors beyond our control, such as climate, which make some regions more attractive than others. There are factors we are learning partially to control, such as atmosphere. There are also such factors as the supply of houses, the conditions of buildings, the quality and character of the built environment, opportunities for shopping and recreation, ease of access, communications with other regions and a host of other considerations that man can control if he wills. These are the factors compelling us to relate regional growth and urban decay to each other, for just as regions where decay is at its worst are unattractive, and discouraging to both the migrant and to the native population, so do they also provide the greatest opportunity for redevelopment in a comprehensive, efficient and attractive way. Furthermore, we have to note that in areas of rapid and concentrated growth, such as parts of Lancashire, South Wales and Middlesbrough in the nineteenth century, and so many of the satellite towns of the London complex during this century, the concentration in time and space of building of similar structure is likely to lead to a concentration of decay. At the moment the great problem of urban renewal is in the North, largely because it was in the North that the great unplanned rapid eruption of urban structures occurred in the nineteenth century. What will be the scale, and the timing, of the great urban renewal of the square miles of semi-detached houses characterising the suburbia of the South-East? Will the problem of renewal be easier or harder if, in the next few decades, an even further intensification of investment takes place in that region, with the inevitable consequences of 'fossilising' the development pattern, so that renewal can mean little other than replication, because restructuring of the region as a whole, or of its separate towns, will be too difficult or too expensive? The scale, direction and type of present investment has an important bearing on the opportunities remaining when the next generation is faced with the decay of towns built by our recent predecessors. Urban investment creates an inertia that expresses itself as a resistance to change and a failure to adapt to modern needs. An over-dense or very costly development over a wide area is likely to strengthen the resistance, and the twenty-first century will be saddled with towns whose basic patterns were conceived in the age of horse-drawn vehicles, nurtured in the age of public urban transport, matured before the impact of the motor-car was fully understood, and fossilised by unimaginative investment and passive acceptance of economic forces.

If there is one inference to be drawn from the chaos of our towns it is that their land-use structure is now, in many cases, outmoded. They suffer from a functional obsolescence, for their design no longer allows them efficiently to fulfil their functions. The inefficient transportation system most evident at rush hours is an indication not so much of a bad traffic system as of an archaic land-use pattern, which locates so many of the buildings to which people want to travel at 9.0 a.m. in one very small part of the town. In medieval times this was convenient and desirable. Is it so today and tomorrow?

This is a question that has lately assumed a greater urgency and importance because of the number of towns now undertaking central-area redevelopment. Far too often these are simply stream-lined versions of the old centre, with rather higher rents demanded for what is only 'chromium-plated half-timbering'. Whether there is need of a different land-use if the town as a whole is to be efficient is rarely considered. Equally rarely mentioned is the impact of the redevelopment on the rest of the town, or on the land-users of the old centre. Even more rarely do we question whether a town should retain a functional centre.

There are many reasons for this failure to face up to the questions we have posed. Perhaps the main reason is that we have not yet made an adequate reassessment of the functions of towns. Some towns obviously fulfil, and should fulfil, different functions than others. To do so, some towns may require centres of one kind, some of another, and some, perhaps, no centre at all. There can be no golden rule. Each town has to be considered not only separately, but also in the context of its region, and in the context of the proposed redevelopments of other towns in that region. The renewal proposals should take account of the possibility of yet another revolution in transport and other urban activities, and of the opportunities that may be presented if the town eventually adopts a new shape, designed not to perpetuate a pattern suited to an earlier age, but to enable the town more easily to fulfil its functions.

None of this is likely to be achieved until the central Government, after consultation with regional planning boards, councils and local authorities, gives a clear lead about how it expects the coming population growth to be distributed between regions. The easy way out is to say that present trends will continue: but that is simply to ape the faint-heartedness of those who felt that violent trade-cycles were inevitable. If we set our sights firmly on a population pattern for thirty years hence, then the introduction of regional variations in investment allowances, housing subsidies, controlled rents, income tax and many other variables within our control will be available as tools to help us to achieve the target. At the same time an integrated transport policy, carefully devised not only to link regions and to stimulate growth, but also to enable the different towns to fulfil their different functions, will be another force on the side of the planners.

Once such a policy has been established, there will be need for the regional planning boards and councils to look at the towns within their regions, and to assess how they can best be developed. This will involve a reassessment of their functions, but should result in a more efficient use of our investment resources and a reduction in needless expenditure of effort and time in travelling. In the areas where decay is greatest, the opportunities to act in this way will also be great. If, however, our decaying towns are now redeveloped in a way that ignores the need for a rethinking of their functions, the problems of the future will exceed those known to us, and the cost of solution will be enormous.

If, then, we turn to the problem of how to cope with our present decay, we should realise that in our very proper concern with the importance of doing something, we should try to ensure that what we do makes sense in the long run.

This remark has to be taken in at least two very important contexts. One is that, having so far failed to produce a national policy, a compatible set of regional policies and a well-considered urban policy, we should admit the urgent need for these and get on with producing them. At the same time we should try to deal with our present problems in a way that gives greatest opportunity to our planners to evolve forward-looking policies at national, regional and local levels.

The second context in which we should frame any fundamental attitude is that of household formation and the brief but important reduction we expect to see in the demand for additional houses. We have already explained that this provides us with an important opportunity for renewal.

Within these two contexts, of the need for a positive regional policy and the shape of household formation, we have to formulate a policy about urban decay. Part of this policy has already been advocated. It is that in our planning and legislation we should try to ensure that, if decay appears as a consequence of our actions, then it is by design and deliberate choice rather than by accident. But this takes no account of the decay that already exists, either to a degree that makes it obvious to everybody or to a lesser degree, when expenditure on repairs and maintenance is only just beginning to be too low to keep pace with the wear and tear time must always bring. This is the matter to which we now turn.

In most countries, housing policy has slowly changed since the end of the war, when the emphasis was largely on the provision of as many new houses as was possible, the repair of war-damaged houses and the control of rents. As the shortage of housing eased, it became possible to abolish or to reduce rent control in most countries and to pay increasing attention to urban renewal. In Britain this has had two principal features. There has been demolition of unfit houses and an attempt to improve existing houses, but the word 'improvement' has acquired a special meaning, which we explain below. There has been little attention to repairs and maintenance that do not result in improvement, defined in this sense.

The picture may be seen more clearly if we look briefly at what has been done and at some of the post-war legislation. Until about 1955 there had been negligible slum-clearance since before the war, but since that date about 800,000 houses had been cleared in Great Britain by the middle of 1967. In recent years, demolition or closing of slum houses has been proceeding at around 75,000–80,000 each year. About two-thirds of these have been in clearance areas. Formal action by local authorities has also resulted in about 30,000 unfit houses being reconditioned each year.

These figures have to be considered in the knowledge that local authorities have a statutory duty to deal with unfit houses, either by clearance or by reconditioning.

Another statutory duty of local authorities is to provide 'standard grants' to owners of houses built before 1945, and judged still to have fifteen years of useful life, for the provision of certain basic amenities. Details of this duty are given in Appendix 9. All we need to note here is that, provided the house meets the requirements just mentioned and is being improved up to a specified standard, then any owner has the right to a grant from the local authority. This grant will not exceed half of the cost of the improvements, and in some cases may be less than this. Local authorities can also obtain money from the Exchequer to help them to improve any of their own houses falling into a similar category.

Apart from these statutory duties, the local authorities have discretionary powers. One of these, introduced in 1949, enables the authority to make a grant towards the cost of improving a house up to the standard one might reasonably expect to find in a modern house. In normal cases the authority has to be satisfied that such a house is likely to have a useful life of at least thirty years, although in some exceptional cases a shorter life-expectancy is permitted. These grants may also be made for conversions of houses into flats.

Some local authorities are more inclined to use these discretionary powers than are others. Whether the grant is 'standard' or 'discretionary', the local authority can recover three-quarters of the cost from the Exchequer. Recently improvement grants have been made at the rate of about 120,000–130,000 each year. Well over a million houses have been improved with their aid.

Another important power, used more by some authorities than by others, is that of requiring property-owners to ensure that their houses have the basic amenities. In any area a tenant may ask the local authority to force the landlord to take the necessary action. A landlord may obtain a grant towards the cost, and the authority is also required to offer a loan to the owner to assist him with his share of the cost. The owner may, if he wishes, require the local authority to purchase the house from him at a fair price. If he does not wish to sell and is unwilling to install the five basic amenities, then the council may do their work at their own expense and recover the cost from the owner. The work does not proceed without the consent of the tenant.

All of these powers relate either to the provisions of basic amenities or to raising a house to 'modern' standards or to conversion into flats or other self-contained units. They do not cover repairs. Local authorities can enforce repairs to unfit houses, but only up to the stage where the house can be lifted out of the demolition class, and then only if the expense is reasonable. They can also deal with specific repairs that are necessary if statutory nuisances are to be abated. Finally, they have powers to lend money to individual owners who wish to make repairs, in much the same way as building societies sometimes do.

There has been frequent comment that despite these grants and loan schemes many property-owners, including owner-occupiers, have not attempted to improve their houses by providing the basic amenities. There are many reasons for this. While some local authorities have advertised the schemes very widely, others have not, or they have done so in ineffective ways. But this is not the whole story. Some people are content to live as they do, without all of these amenities. Some would like to see them provided, but do not feel able to put up with the inconvenience of having builders in the house for, possibly, several days or even weeks. Other owners feel that although they can obtain a grant for perhaps half of the cost, and (in some cases) a loan to cover at least part of the rest, the gain to them as owners is insufficient. Even though they may receive increased rent, they feel that if they have money to invest the most profitable outlet is not the improvement of their houses. Owner-occupiers sometimes argue similarly, and also point out that if they improve their houses then they may also have to pay higher rates on them.

It would be wrong to infer that the reasons we have just listed have prevented progress. The City of Leeds provides one example of a town in which there has been notable success. Using its powers to designate improvement areas, in which all houses must be brought up to standard, subject only to the avoidance of hardship to elderly or infirm occupiers, the local authority had listed sixty-six improvement areas between July 1955 and October 1966. In them were 13,000 houses. Over 7000 of these were either satisfactory before the area was designated or were brought up to standard through improvement grants. Some 1600 houses were acquired by the local authority in the process. Other cities and towns have made similar progress.

The facts remain that there is still a great deal to be done, and that many house-owners do not appear to want to spend money on improvement. It is also perfectly clear to anybody who walks along streets of houses built between the wars or earlier that many owners are not spending enough money on repairs. Some local authorities, as well as private landlords and owner-occupiers, have houses that are clearly decaying.

In Chapter 5 we outlined a theory of obsolescence and decay in which we introduced 'the state of decay' when the owner of a building would decide that the most profitable thing for him to do—taking account not only of immediate profit, but also of such factors as his desire for liquidity—would be for him to spend nothing on the property. In practice, maintenance expenditures are of many kinds. An owner may consider that he should replace a broken pane of glass, because the cost of the repair is trivial compared with the consequences of damp, but that he should not repoint the brick work, because the cost of this is too high when compared with the benefits. He might also argue that it is easier to live in, or to let, a house with slightly deficient pointing than one with a few missing window-panes. One way or another, and often incorrectly, he weighs the cost of a repair against the benefits he expects to derive from it.

If this is correct, then it would seem that one way of encouraging owners to keep their houses in reasonable repair would be to reduce the cost. Another would be to increase the benefits of repair. Is there a way of doing this?

Until 1963 owners of houses were taxed under Schedule A. From that year, owner-occupiers have ceased to be taxed on the notional income they have derived through being able to live in their houses rent-free. Landlords are taxed under Schedule D on their net income, after allowing for management, repairs and other expenses. We can usefully spend a few moments looking at some of the implications of this arrangement.

Under Schedule A an owner-occupier who was able to produce bills incurred through repairing and maintaining his house was able to set the total (or the average over a period of years) against his notional Schedule A income. If his repair expenditure was high enough he could completely escape Schedule A tax. In many cases people did not take advantage of this concession, partly because of ignorance and partly because of the trouble that was involved in keeping and producing bills. When owner-occupiers did take advantage of it, they effectively repaired their houses at less than current costs. Now that Schedule A liability has been abolished, all owner-occupiers are to a certain extent subsidised, but they obtain no direct tax relief for repairs and maintenance. One incentive to repair has gone.

Landlords are able to set their repair bills against income, but, as Miss Nevitt has ably pointed out, the landlord is given no depreciation allowance on his property, and consequently it is rarely a commercial proposition to spend much either improving or maintaining property with an expected remaining life of less than twenty or so years.[3]

Before people spend money, two conditions have to exist. The money has to be available (or, at least, expected), while there also has to be some inducement to spend it in that particular way. If we wish, as a community, to encourage spending on repairs, then we can do so by making the money available and providing some incentive. One possibility is to enact that any owner wishing to borrow money in order to bring his house up to a certain standard of repair may do so from the local authority, possibly at favourable rates of interest. This may mean that the owner is being subsidised. In the past he has often provided the subsidy. We need to look anew at our housing and consider whether it may not be in the national interest now to subsidise the maintenance of our housing stock. Doing so may in the long run be cheaper than subsidising new building.

If the money is made available in this way, so that both the landlord and the owner-occupier can, if necessary, borrow the money that is needed for repairs, then one of the conditions we have just mentioned is fulfilled. The remaining condition is that there should be some incentive in this way. For the owner-occupier there has been no direct incentive since the abolition of Schedule A assessments. Two similar solutions come to mind. Each presents difficulties, but each may be capable of slight modification that will make it practicable.

One could give all owner-occupiers a house-allowance, to be set against their earned income-tax liability. This allowance could be granted automatically provided that the house was kept in reasonable repair. Local-authority inspectors could visit houses they suspected of being in substandard repair and, where necessary, issue notices of disrepair, which would immediately deprive the owner-occupier of his house-allowance unless he could produce bills totalling a certain amount over the last few years. Such a scheme need not involve the annual, or even the triennial, inspection of every house, and, although it would probably mean adding to the army of local-authority employees, their cost might become trivial compared with the gain in the quality of housing. At the same time we could introduce depreciation-allowances for all owners, be they owner-occupiers or landlords.

A variation on this scheme is that the rateable value of houses should be increased, and that owners should be made liable for the payment of rates. At the moment the liability is usually with the occupier. The rate charged would have a rebate for all property in good repair, and the system of inspection just described could be adopted. The advantages of this scheme is that it would be easier for the rebates to be varied locally if this seemed to be necessary because of local conditions. Landlords unable to collect the rates from their tenants, but able to provide proof of an effort to do so, could ask the local authority to take action against the tenant. Another advantage is that owners who do not pay income tax would still receive an incentive to keep their property in reasonable repair.

Proposals such as these are bound to meet with opposition, and it is highly unlikely that they would work without some modification, but they are worth considering. They provide a source of funds out of which owners may borrow in order to repair their houses and also incentives (or penalties) designed to encourage the use of this fund. There is the carrot and the stick. If there are doubts about their usefulness, they could be tried out in a small group of towns or a single region.

We can no longer postpone an attempt to answer the question about the relative merits of renewal and repair. 'Urban renewal' is now a catch-phrase, which seems to mean extensive demolition of property, most of it old, in a way that clears a large area of ground and so permits the planning and construction of a new set of buildings, streets and spaces. Usually it takes place in or close to a town centre, or in some other place where there is a cluster of old buildings. Sometimes renewal policies stem from a desire to deal with a housing problem. A second frequent aim is to provide new shops and/or offices, usually with improved parking facilities. The solution of a traffic problem is sometimes the main aim. A fourth impetus to renewal is an attempt to provide a better environment. It is, of course, true that there may be other reasons for renewal, but these seem to be the main reasons. It is also true that very often these aims can be achieved in a variety of ways, but that renewal is chosen.

Urban renewal and the housing problem interact at two levels. There is usually a displacement of families from houses to be demolished, and the provision of alternative accommodation for them. Apart from this, the renewal programme, taken as a whole, requires resources that may also be required for building additional houses to provide for new families.

In deciding upon a policy we must not be concerned simply with the physical conditions of houses. We must also consider the environment. This is not simply an expression of aesthetic prejudices, for it is also a statement of an economic fact. The quality of the environment, admittedly not easy to measure, affects property values directly; and because owners or occupiers of properties seem only rarely to try to improve their own houses beyond the standard set by the environment, a cumulative downward trend of appearance and maintenance expenditures often hastens the onset of severe decay, and so a further fall in value. Our survey found that once a certain stage of physical decay had been reached, there was a strong correlation between further decay and poor environment. Chapter 3 has emphasised the links between physical decay and sociological factors.

Old Houses into New Homes announces that a greater share of public housing expenditure should go to the improvement of older houses, and it describes legislative changes designed to encourage owners of houses to spend more on bringing them up to acceptable standards and keeping them there. The need to improve environments is also emphasised, and there are provisions for the Government to assist in the cost.

Let us begin by looking at it in purely economic terms. The question of when it becomes 'more economic' to demolish and rebuild rather than to improve is one that has been tackled at several levels. An interesting opportunity to ask it arose in the preparation of the Teesside Survey and Plan, which began under the direction of Franklin Medhurst, with J. Parry Lewis as a consultant. It was based on a full-scale Survey of Housing and Environmental Deficiency (SHED), which enabled us to allot marks to describe the overall condition of housing and environment, zone by zone.

Examination of the costs of various remedial work showed that it would cost approximately £30 per SHED point to bring a house up to acceptable standards. A first use of SHED was thus to provide a rough estimate of the cost of rehabilitation, zone by zone. In this context we were thinking simply of repair and improvement costs, and excluding all social and secondary costs, but including expenditure on environmental improvement.

We then argued that the function of a house is to provide services, such as shelter, and it is from these services that it derives its value as a building. It is reasonable to argue that as the years pass the value of these services (measured in real terms) will slowly depreciate, as tastes and standards rise while the ageing house slowly decays. Furthermore, because we place a lower present value on the prospect of shelter in ten years' time than we do on the certainty of it now, the stream of future services from a house should be discounted at an appropriate rate of interest. Thus, if a house provides services currently valued at V per annum and is expected to last for n years, then its present value is not nV but, say, hV, where $hV = V + (1-d-r) V + (1-d-r)^2 V + -$ where there is one term for each year, where d is the percentage rate of depreciation in the sense just described, and r is a rate of interest.

We also considered that a rehabilitated house would probably never be quite as good as a new house of similar size, that it would probably depreciate faster than a new house, and that it would survive for less long.

Assumptions of this kind enabled us to argue in the following terms. It costs £x to demolish an old house and to build a new house. The result is a new house whose present value is some multiple (say h) of V, the unknown value of new, good-standard accommodation. It also costs £y to rehabilitate this old house, and it will provide shelter for a shorter period. Its present value is a multiple (k) of V where k has been obtained by use of the same formula, but with different numbers in it. We thus have

	Cost	Present value of result
Demolished and redeveloped	x	hV
Rehabilitated	y	kV

A rule to help the decision-maker is that if

$$\frac{y}{x} \text{ is less than } \frac{k}{h}$$

it is better value for money to improve the existing house, but if the reverse is true then redevelopment gives better value.

As an example, suppose that, just after the money has been spent on it, an improved house provides services worth 80 per cent of the service a new house would provide. Let it depreciate quickly, becoming only 50 per cent as good as a new house before it is scrapped in fifteen years' time. Let the new house depreciate more slowly, taking a hundred years to reach this low level. Take a 6 per cent discount rate, related to interest rates. Calculations on the above lines, and using these assumptions, which are clearly biased in favour of redevelopment rather than improvement, show that, provided the cost of improvement is not more than 56 per cent of the cost of redevelopment, then improvement gives the better value.

The knowledge of the SHED scores, and so of the approximate rehabilitation costs, on a zonal basis, thus enables the new Teesside Borough to determine fairly quickly the areas where demolition is the best 'economic' proposition and where some form of at least partial conservation may present better value for money.

It is interesting to make a rough appraisal of the national situation in these terms. *Old Houses into New Homes* presents the estimates of repair costs shown in Table 10.

If we take £3000 as the cost of a new house, and make assumptions so favourable to redevelopment that the critical value of k/h is not

TABLE 10. ESTIMATES OF REPAIR COSTS, ENGLAND AND WALES, 1967

Repair costs	Unfit dwellings (000)	Dwellings not unfit (000)	All dwellings
under £125	20	10,112	10,132
£125–249	136	2,385	2,521
£250–499	414	914	1,328
£500–999	590	379	969
£1000 and over	676	74	750
TOTAL	1,836	13,864	15,700

as high as 56 per cent, but is as low as 33 per cent, then it would be a better-value proposition to redevelop only 750,000 houses. The rest, including nearly two-thirds of our unfit houses, would be more appropriately improved if the situation were assessed simply on this narrow basis. This estimate ignores the houses that would cost less than £1000 to repair, but more than £1000 to repair and to bring up to standard in respect of internal amenities. It seems likely that the effect of this would be to add not more than 250,000 houses to the number to be redeveloped.

This kind of argument is relevant whether it is an owner-occupier considering whether to demolish and rebuild his own house or to improve it, or a large landlord (public or private) with some collective scheme in mind. But once we start to consider groups of houses, the importance of other arguments grows. As so often happens when a decision rule is formulated, it would be all too easy to use this idea as an excuse for the lack of considered judgement. 'Rules' such as these should never be more than pointers, summarising the logical implication of one set of facts and assumptions, but always used in the knowledge that other questions have also to be asked, and that there will rarely be a case in which there is one answer right by every criterion. Even, indeed, on economic grounds, the better-value action may be wrong. It could, for example, mean postponing new building for a few years and then finding that an immense demand has piled up, crying out for attention at a time when other demands are also arising. In this way it could lead to an exaggeration of fluctuations in building activity, which would be harmful to both the building industry and the general economy. This is particularly important in view of the shape of household formation in the seventies. The shifting of public-sector policy towards rehabilitation will imply a further reduction in the load on the house-building industry. Yet in the later seventies and throughout the eighties household formation will rise, and by then growing incomes will also be adding substantially to demand. Much redevelopment of recent years— and even today—may be condemned both for failing the value-for-money test and for overstraining our resources. But in a few years' time the dip in demand for new houses will present us with a brief golden opportunity to adapt our towns in ways that will not be excessively constrained by scarce building-resources. We should now be preparing our programmes ready for a phased introduction as other demands decline.

Before looking at other reasons for not being too concerned with a purely micro-economic decision rule, we may glance at the renewal of buildings other than houses. It is true that houses form the majority of our buildings and occupy most of our built urban land, but in our urban centres many redevelopment schemes mean the demolition of very little housing. Shops and offices are more commonly the subject of the central-redevelopment proposals. An important difference is that whereas most housing-renewal schemes stem from local-authority initiative, many central-area schemes initiate in private proposals. For shops and offices there is some provision in public schemes, but the piecemeal renewal characterising most of our centres is usually private, and so are many of the larger schemes. Housing to rent, on the other hand, is not an attractive proposal for private money, although the disappearance of rent control and the gradual approach of 'fair rents' to market rents may yet reverse the trend away from the private provision of houses to rent.

Chapter 4 has described some of the processes of change in an office and shopping area. In most cases the victim is the small business. The new development provides premises at several times the rent that has been paid for the old premises, and often the original occupier cannot pay them.

Sometimes it is argued that those who suffer when the small firms are driven out of business are the inefficient. It is time, people say, that Tesco and Wimpey drove out the corner shop and the putter-on of chimney-pots. But technical efficiency and business efficiency are two different concepts, the latter depending as much on book-keeping practice, debt-collection and borrowing skill as on the efficient use of labour, materials and equipment. The small business plays an important part in the social and economic life of the community. If we redevelop in a way that pays scant regard to it, then in the end the community pays the price, either by having higher rents passed onto it, in the form of higher charges, or by having to walk farther to the nearest shop, or by having to pay the costs of improved road and motor access.

The whole point is that redevelopment, traffic control and the other instruments of policy are still in search of the policy they should serve. Do we want neat new buildings, with traffic on the move? Or do we want to adapt our towns to new possibilities and new needs in a way that takes account of what is virtuous in the old?

We have seen how traffic legislation or redevelopment in one part of a town may stimulate demand for the occupation of property in another part; how planning uncertainties may accelerate decay; how local-traffic problems may lead to vacancies; how old properties may, by their cheapness, attract a useful range of tenants; and how properties that cannot be easily adapted may become empty and eventually derelict.

Unfortunately these very obvious points are often ignored when urban decisions are taken. Here we must include not only redevelopment decisions, but many other kinds of decision, such as those involving parking regulations, traffic flows, school locations, and so on. Action designed to affect some feature of a town may set up a chain of reactions that can easily completely alter some other aspects of a remote place, possibly, even in a different town. Urban legislators frequently legislate for traffic without considering the impact on accessibility, trade, rents, maintenance expenditures and physical condition. Even less rarely do they consider the impact of their actions on urban activities beyond their own local-authority boundaries. Yet in all of these ways the rate of urban decay is being affected. It is, indeed, quite common for an attempt 'to deal with decay' in one area to produce decay in another.

This neglect of the interdependencies defining our urban system sometimes spells ruin for the redevelopment itself. It is not uncommon for two or more central-area shopping schemes to proceed in near-by areas, each expecting to draw custom from the other's area. Even more common is the failure to appreciate that new buildings cannot often be let for rents anything like as low as those they are intended to replace; and so the net result is sometimes the replacing of busy, decrepit shops by splendid, empty shells.

The late Victorian industrial cottage converted into a cobbler's shop may be an ideal form of accommodation for the user and be located in a place very convenient for the surrounding resident or working population. It may be condemned as ugly or as occupying land 'needed' for other purposes, and these are perfectly valid arguments in favour of demolition; but they must be weighed against other arguments.

A well-distributed and suitably located stock of ageing property can, under certain circumstances, provide cheap and adequate accommodation in a way that fulfils a useful social function. If this property were not under the threat of being compulsorily acquired and demolished at short notice, then much of it would often be in better repair. But if it is demolished and replaced with new buildings of a similar description, then the new rents, related to current building costs, will usually mean that there is a totally different kind of occupier or that the old occupier has to charge more for his services.

This last point applies equally to housing. The houses that are knocked down often tend to house communities far from representative of the larger community in whose name, and by whose standards, the action is taken. Those provided in their place may or may not be suitable in design and location for the displaced tenants or owner-occupiers, but it is almost certain that they will be let at rents far greater than those the tenants have previously paid. It may be argued that in cases of hardship various forms of assistance may be obtained; but there will still be many who, through public action, will lose the opportunity to live at 'lower' standards and to pay lower rents than 'the public' considers to be 'proper'. It is partly on these grounds that we may favour maintenance and improvement. It need not divide the existing community, or alter the basic established physical relationships between spaces to which the people have become accustomed, and which they have absorbed into their lives. And it can often be done in a way that will not lead to large increases in rent.

There has been space to touch on only a few of the factors that should be taken into account in deciding between redevelopment and rehabilitation. The immense possibilities that only redevelopment can bring, but which may often be lost through bad planning, must be remembered and taken into account when decisions are being reached. One must also consider not only the frequently tabulated costs and benefits, but also the incidence of these costs and benefits. For too long we have been party to redevelopment whose costs have fallen unfairly on other authorities, on property-owners or on small businessmen. It is some recognition of this that underlies the Government's proposal to increase compensation to certain owner-occupiers and private landlords whose houses are demolished under slum-clearance orders. But the small businessman is still ill-favoured; and so, sometimes, is the small local authority.

There is no single rule for deciding how to solve an urban problem. What is important is that alternative solutions should each be submitted to a variety of tests, so that in reaching one's decisions one does so in full awareness of what the answer would be if this or that test were dominant. In this way one will know more precisely what it is that one is choosing and rejecting. It also means that each problem will be considered on its own merits. We have too often begun to deal with an urban problem by commissioning a redevelopment scheme rather than a solution; and the federal bulldozer has cleared the ground for the erection of a costly monument testifying to our failure to ask the right questions. Now we must be careful that 'improvement' does not become another catch-phrase.

There will be times when the best policy for an area may be to improve parts of it and to redevelop other parts, in a way that marries old and new. To think that 'improvement' can be applied to all the properties over a large area can be as wrong as thinking that every property should be redeveloped. It is the whole town that needs to be improved, possibly through a mixture of means, including demolition, rebuilding and rehabilitation. As our towns grow larger and older, and as the demands we make on them change, our problem is to adapt them to our new needs, by whatever means seem best, bearing in mind our spatial, social and economic resources. If we must have a catch-phrase, could it be 'urban adaptation based on urban understanding'.

Urban decay has no single cause, and a policy towards it must have many threads. We have argued that it is part of urban change, and that there is much about its causation and effects that we do not understand. This is one reason for doing more urban research and measurement. Even without this we can reduce the creation of decay by accident if we think more often of the town as a complex of interdependent spaces, functions and activities, such that change in any one of them may create change in others. Changes outside the town may have equally important effects, and just as policy towards decay should be part of a larger urban policy (which should include an urban housing policy), so should urban policy, taking account of the differing needs of different towns, be part of a regional policy. But decisions about whether to spend on repairs or to give the forces of decay a free hand are taken by millions of individual people and a comparatively small number of corporate bodies. These are decisions that can be influenced by measures such as we have proposed. A policy combining these points, so that on the one hand we take urban and regional decisions against a background of greater study and understanding, and on the other facilitate and encourage expenditure on repair, can help us to solve a problem that only recently has been admitted to our consciousness. However correct our housing legislation has been in the past to meet problems of the past, and however desirable our traffic policies and taxation schemes have been in the interests of particular ends, we should now look afresh at them all, and devise policies and legislation that will enable us to change our towns into well-kept, pleasant and efficient places. Our policies must look forward toward our aims, rather than confusedly towards our more obvious present problems considered in isolation.

The Indices of Physical Condition and Environmental Quality

The methods used in the Manchester–Salford–Stretford survey are outlined in Chapter 2. The purpose of this appendix is to give more detail about the selection of observation points and the composition of the indices and about the reliability of the results.

Selection of Buildings

In the original study the area was divided into forty-one squares of two-kilometre side. From tables of random numbers forty-nine pairs of numbers lying between 0 and 199 were selected. These were combined to yield the Cartesian co-ordinates of forty-nine points, which were marked on a template, and which fitted a two-kilometre square of a large-scale map. It was possible to cover any given square in eight different ways, depending on which edge of the template was along its northern boundary and which face was uppermost. For each square we selected a digit between 1 and 8 at random to determine the way in which the template should be put on that square. The points were then marked on the map.

In a later study of Ashton-under-Lyne the method of choosing buildings was rather different. First, it was concerned only with residential decay, thus no index of environmental decay was produced for points studied, and non-residential buildings were ignored. Secondly, as explained below, the random-sampling method employed was related more directly to enumeration-district boundaries, since it had been found useful to compare the results of the first survey with certain census results. Thirdly, the sample taken was significantly larger than that taken in the first survey.

In the first instance it was decided to take a 1 per cent sample of

residences in Ashton-under-Lyne. The number of residences in each
of the enumeration districts of Ashton was obtained from the 1961
census data, and hence the number of residences to be taken to
ensure a 1 per cent sample from each enumeration district was
determined. The boundaries of the enumeration districts were then
drawn on a six-inch Ordnance Survey map. A template was constructed to cover a one-kilometre square. This template was divided
into nine equal squares, and nine numbered co-ordinates were obtained from a table of random numbers for each small square. The
position of the template, for each one-kilometre square on the map,
was likewise randomly determined. Thus for each one-kilometre
square eighty-one points were plotted. Nine of them (one from each
small square) were numbered 1, nine of them 2, and so on. Then
for each enumeration district the predetermined number of houses
was selected by taking those houses on which the random points
fell (or, more accurately, those within twenty metres of a random
point), taking first those random points numbered 1, then those
numbered 2, and so on. Where an insufficient number of points were
to be found in a particular enumeration district, a second position
for the template was taken at random, and so on, until the requisite
number of houses had been obtained.

Two comments must be made on this method. Firstly, houses on
the corners of streets had a slightly higher chance of being selected
than others. This may have introduced a small amount of bias, for
pubs tend to be located on street corners, and also to be kept in
better repair than other residences in their area. Secondly, in areas
where there has been much recent (i.e. post-1961) development, the
use of the 1961 figures for each enumeration district involved a
certain amount of bias against post-1961 houses.

A second sample was taken for reasons explained below. The same
observer looked at the southern part of Oldham (census area B),
this time taking a 3 per cent sample, but in such a way that it could
be broken down into its three 1 per cent components.

The Composition of the Indices

Our observers were asked to note whether there was 'none', 'some',
'little', or 'much' of the attributes listed in Table A1.1. Clearly, if
we had employed a large number of students, there could have been
independent checking of observations, and an attempt could have

been made to eliminate observer bias. But there were few students of sufficient calibre who were available in the Christmas vacation. Consequently we had to try to reduce bias before it began, by carefully instructing the observers and attempting to indicate how much of an attribute would still be described as 'little'.

Our next task was to combine their observations into a mark. After trying various more sophisticated schemes, four of us eventually sat down and argued out the following scheme of marks for physical condition (a high mark being bad condition). We felt that little surface deterioration was worth about the same mark as a little broken glazing. A little timber rot was more serious, and perhaps equivalent to some peeling paint. At the other end of the scale, and to illustrate our attempt to make the marks additive, we felt that much sagging roof was about equivalent to some settlement plus some timber rot. There are obvious criticisms of our scheme: but we felt that it was worth trying.

TABLE A1.1. WEIGHTS USED IN INDEX OF PHYSICAL CONDITION

	Much	Some	Little	None
Surface deterioration	5	3	1	0
Paint peeling	3	2	1	0
Displaced roof units	9	5	1	0
Broken glazing	7	3	1	0
Gutter-/down-pipe leaking	7	3	1	0
Settlement evident	11	6	3	0
Timber rot	8	4	2	0
Sagging roof	10	6	2	0

We adopted a similar scheme for the environment, as shown in Table A1.2.

TABLE A1.2. WEIGHTS USED IN INDEX OF ENVIRONMENTAL CONDITION

	Much	Some	Little	None
Offensive smells	3	2	1	0
Air pollution	3	2	1	0
Noise	3	2	1	0
Grass or trees	0	1	2	3
Litter	3	2	1	0
Parked vehicles	3	2	1	0

Reliability of Results

There are two sources of error. There may be observer prejudice, either because of different observers, or because the same observer may vary his standards from day to day or from one type of housing to another. It is also possible that the sample size is inadequate.

We have not had the resources to do much investigation of these matters, but the following points may be made:

1. The smoothness of the curves in Figures 1, 5 and 6 (pp. 11, 17, 18) and the high correlations with census data encourages us to have some faith in our methods, especially for larger areas.

2. The Ashton-under-Lyne study involved two independent samples (by the same observer) of 1 per cent of the houses. The study of part of Oldham was based on three 1 per cent samples. The results are summarised in Figures A1.1 and A1.2. Clearly, the combined 3 per cent sample is more likely to be reliable than is any single 1 per cent sample. The actual reliability depends on the absolute (rather than the percentage) sample size. The Oldham study suggests that a sample of 140 houses (corresponding to 1 per cent) is too small to be

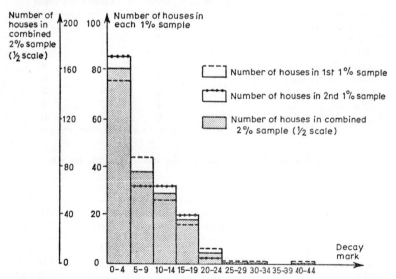

Figure A1.1. Histograms showing frequency of occurrence of each range of decay marks in each 1 per cent sample, and in the combined 2 per cent sample, of houses in the Ashton-under-Lyne survey

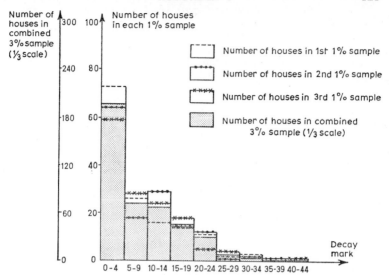

Figure A1.2. Histograms showing frequency of occurrence of each range of decay marks in each 1 per cent sample, and in the 3 per cent sample in the Oldham survey

safe: but a sample treble this size produces results that accord well with those of the larger survey of Manchester.

Correlation Coefficients

Table A1.3 shows the square-by-square correlation of the two indices for the forty-one points in the main study. It is important to keep in mind the caution made on pages 18–21. Some of the correlation coefficients mean very little, not because of their magnitude, but because of the distributions of the individual values of x and y.

Subsequent Developments

The indices described in this appendix were modified under the direction of the authors when they were associated with Teesside Survey and Plan. In this work a single index of housing and environmental deficiency was compiled, and was used to evaluate probable levels of expenditure needed to bring houses up to acceptable standards. The study, known as SHED (Survey of Housing and Environmental Deficiency), is more fully described in the report of Teesside Survey and Plan.

TABLE A1.3. INDICES OF PHYSICAL CONDITION AND ENVIRONMENT:
MEANS, CONFIDENCE LIMITS AND CORRELATION

Square	No. of buildings	Mean value of index of decay (x)	Mean value of index of Adverse environment (y)	95 Confidence % x	limits for y	Correlation between x and y
1	18	9·1	4·8	±5·6	±1·1	0·46
2	23	6·8	4·8	3·3	0·7	−0·07
3	23	4·4	5·6	2·3	0·7	0·13
4	34	5·6	6·2	2·2	0·8	−0·06
5	35	7·1	6·0	3·0	0·6	0·45
6	37	16·4	8·0	4·5	0·9	0·39
7	39	3·4	4·6	0·9	0·7	0·52
8	40	4·1	4·5	1·8	0·5	0·15
9	37	12·3	7·3	1·8	0·9	0·29
10	41	10·2	9·4	2·2	0·6	0·38
11	39	13·3	8·2	4·7	0·6	0·51
12	31	10·7	11·3	4·3	0·8	0·27
13	31	7·2	5·7	4·5	0·3	0·74
14	41	10·3	7·8	3·1	0·3	0·00
15	36	11·5	9·6	3·3	0·5	−0·20
16	47	10·1	9·4	4·4	0·5	0·67
17	40	5·9	9·9	2·7	0·6	0·61
18	41	15·4	8·5	4·0	0·8	0·05
19	33	8·3	8·4	2·8	0·8	−0·48
20	33	4·1	7·9	1·2	0·8	0·06
21	39	6·3	6·1	2·4	0·8	0·24
22	42	9·2	6·4	3·1	0·7	0·62
23	47	7·2	8·2	2·3	0·5	0·36
24	43	9·8	7·2	3·0	0·7	0·35
25	35	9·3	6·7	3·0	0·6	0·22
26	37	6·8	9·1	2·0	0·8	0·09
27	38	4·3	5·2	2·1	0·6	0·39
28	34	1·0	5·3	0·4	0·6	0·28
29	25	5·7	4·7	1·7	0·6	0·03
30	18	3·0	5·7	1·5	0·9	−0·23
31	22	6·3	3·2	5·7	0·4	−0·06
32	15	4·1	6·3	2·3	0·5	0·03
33	41	3·5	5·7	1·3	0·6	0·09
34	30	3·5	5·1	1·2	0·6	−0·07
35	19	4·8	5·0	3·8	0·8	−0·11
36	23	4·1	5·4	1·4	0·9	−0·01
37	33	0·9	4·1	1·1	0·4	0·18
38	34	2·4	4·8	0·6	0·4	0·17
39	36	3·0	3·8	1·7	0·4	0·44
40	36	1·1	4·1	0·4	0·5	0·27
41	23	3·5	5·3	0·7	0·6	0·41

Description of Land-users in Lower Deansgate at time of First Survey

The tables in this appendix contain the statistics on which the first few pages of Chapter 4 are based.

TABLE A2.1. LAND-USE AND BUILDING CONDITION

Condition	Public buildings	Offices	Shops	Ware-houses	Industry	TOTAL
Good	7	128	34	3	9	181
Fair	8	54	44	23	22	151
Poor	3	15	35	14	34	101
TOTAL	18	197	113	40	65	433

TABLE A2.2. LAND-USE AND DURATION OF STAY

Date of arrival	Public buildings	Offices	Shops	Ware-houses	Industry	TOTAL
1958–62	3	83	24	10	9	129
1945–57	1	55	28	11	26	121
1920–44	4	38	27	7	13	89
before 1920	7	7	14	6	8	42
?	3	14	20	6	9	52
TOTAL	18	197	113	40	65	433

Former location areas

(See Tables A2.3, A2.6, A2.8 and A2.9. Figure A2.1 shows former location areas 1, 2 and 3.)

  0 no former location
  1 Central Manchester area

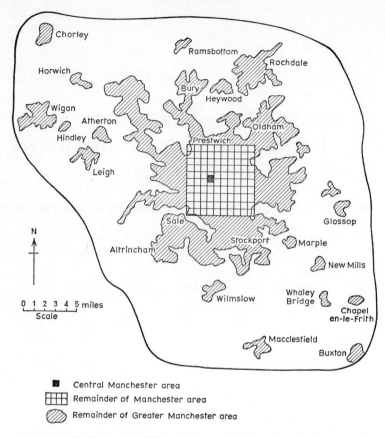

Figure A2.1. Former location areas for firms in Lower Deansgate survey (See also Tables A2.3, A2.6, A2.8 and A2.9)

2 remainder of Manchester area

3 remainder of Greater Manchester area

4 remainder of North-West (approximately Lancashire, Cheshire and Flintshire)

5 remainder of Northern England (approximately North-West plus the area to the north of a line from Buxton to the Humber)

6 elsewhere

? unknown

TABLE A2.3. Land-use and Former Location

Former location	Public buildings	Offices	Shops	Warehouses	Industry	TOTAL
0	6	56	59	14	23	158
1	5	98	29	20	22	174
2					2	2
3		4	2			6
4		4	1		4	9
5			2		2	4
6		7	2	2	2	13
?	7	28	18	4	10	67
TOTAL	18	197	133	40	65	433

TABLE A2.4. Employment and Building Condition

Condition	1–9 persons	10–49 persons	50 + persons	TOTAL
Good	120	54	7	181
Fair	100	44	7	151
Bad	89	10	2	101
TOTAL	309	108	16	433

TABLE A2.5. Employment and Duration of Stay

Date of arrival	1–9 persons	10–49 persons	50 + persons	TOTAL
1958–62	97	28	4	129
1945–57	95	23	3	121
1920–44	58	28	3	89
before 1920	24	14	4	42
?	35	15	2	52
TOTAL	309	108	16	433

TABLE A2.6. EMPLOYMENT AND FORMER LOCATION

Former location	1–9 persons	10–49 persons	50 + persons	TOTAL
0	121	31	6	158
1	115	54	5	174
2	1	1		2
3	6			6
4	6	3		9
5	4			4
6	9	1	3	13
?	47	18	2	67
TOTAL	309	108	16	433

TABLE A2.7. BUILDING CONDITION AND DURATION OF STAY

Date of arrival	Good	Fair	Bad	TOTAL
1958–62	63	34	32	129
1945–57	45	41	35	121
1920–44	43	34	12	89
before 1920	16	19	7	42
?	14	23	15	52
TOTAL	181	151	101	433

TABLE A2.8. BUILDING CONDITION AND FORMER LOCATION

Former location	Good	Fair	Bad	TOTAL
0	62	60	36	158
1	87	51	36	174
2			2	2
3	2	2	2	6
4	3	3	3	9
5	1	1	2	4
6	4	4	5	13
?	22	30	15	67
TOTAL	181	151	101	433

TABLE A2.9. FORMER LOCATION AND DURATION OF STAY

Date of arrival	0	1	2	3	4	5	6	?	TOTAL
1958–62	47	58		4	4	2	6	8	129
1945–57	41	58	1	2	4	1	5	9	121
1920–44	36	44	1		1	1	1	5	89
before 1920	25	13					1	2	42
?	8	1						43	52
TOTAL	158	174	2	6	9	4	13	67	433

Movement into or out of the Lower Deansgate Area, 1962–4

The following tables contain data relevant to pages 41–2 of the text.

TABLE A3.1. MOVEMENT INTO STUDY AREA, 1962–4

Land-use	Size	Date of entry to former premises	Reasons for movement					Former location
			1	2	3	4	5	
00	A	1930–8	1	2	3	12	13	C
07	A	1939–45	16					c
07	A	—	5, 6					X
07	A	1961	3					a/b
07	D	1950–4	4	7				c
07	A	1961	17	7	12	13		c
11	A	1950–4	4	5	9	12	14	C
11	—	—	17					C
12	E	1959	5, 6	7	9	11, 12		C
13	D	1960	5, 6					C
13	A	1955–8	17					
14	C	1950–4	10	1	2	11, 12	14	C
15	C	before 1930	10					c
15	C	1955–8	5, 6					X
15	B	before 1930	4					C
15	B	1950–4	4					C
15	E	—	5					C
15	B	1960	17					a
15	C	1958	4					C
16	A	1962	7					a
16	A	1960	5, 6					a
16	A	1961	11, 12					
19	B	1955–8	5					C
19	A	—	4					C
19	C	1955–8	5, 6	11	12	16		C
40	A	—	16	4				C
41	—	—	17					C
41	—	—	17					

For key see lists of land-uses, reasons and former location given at end of this appendix.

TABLE A3.2. MOVEMENT WITHIN STUDY AREA, 1962–4

Land-use	Size	Date of entry to former premises	1	2	3	4	5
			— Reasons for movement				
07	B	1959	5	6	7	11	12, 13
08	C	?	4, 5				
15	B	1930–8	9	8	6	2	1
16	A	1962	5				
40	A	1947	4				
41	B	1946–9	4				
70	A	1939–45	12, 13	4			

TABLE A3.3. MOVEMENT FROM STUDY AREA, 1962–4

Land-use	Size	Date of entry to area	1	2	3	4	5	Present location
08	A	1946–9	1	2, 3				a
08	C	1919	1	11, 12				c
12	D	1955–8	6	9	11	12		C
15	—	1961	17					X
15	A	1955–8	11	12, 13	5			C
15	D	1959	5	6	9	11, 12	13	C
15	A	before 1930	10					C
15	D	—	5	6	7	11	12	a
16	A	1959	11, 12					X
40	C	1930–8	5	7	9	11, 12	13	a
40	E	1939–45	1, 12					a
40	A	1930–8	4	6	11	12	14	c
41	D	before 1930	5, 6	11	12	13		c
41	A	1928	1					a
70	A	1939–45	4					X
70	E	1963	12	13, 14	1	2		a
70	B	1930–8	11	12, 13	1	2	5, 6	X

KEY TO TABLES

		Land-uses
00	Shops	Grocer; baker/confectioner; sweets/tobacco; butcher; fishmonger; greengrocer; wines, etc.
07		Hardware; domestic, shop or office equipment, furniture, radio, etc., paint, timber.
08		Motors, motor-cycles, accessories, caravans, etc.
11	Offices	Solicitor/barrister
12		Insurance
13		Architect, surveyor, estate agent, auctioneer, consulting engineer
14		Accountant
15		Company office/sales office
16		Professional service
19		Miscellaneous
40	Industries	Light manufacturing/engineering
41		Service
70	Warehouses	Wholesale

Size	
	Number of persons employed
A	fewer than 5
B	5–9
C	10–19
D	20–49
E	50 or more

Former location	
C	Central Manchester
c	Inner ring of decay
X	Rest of Manchester
a	Manchester region
b	North-West England

Reasons for Moving

1. The rent at former premises was raised.
2. The rates at former premises were raised.
3. Business profits no longer justified the rent.
4. The building occupied was cleared or scheduled to be cleared.
5. The building was too small because business had expanded.
6. There was no room for expansion at former site.
7. The building could not be adapted to suit new processes.
8. The landlord was unwilling to do repairs.
9. The building was in a poor condition.
10. The premises were too large and it was uneconomical to remain there.
11. Parking was difficult at former location for staff.
12. Parking was difficult at former location for callers.
13. The congestion at former location made it difficult for goods vehicles to unload.
14. The area was declining and had become unsuitable for the trade/business/profession.
15. The firms with whom firm dealt frequently moved from the area.
16. The lease ended and firm could not renew it.
17. Other reason.

Trip-generation in Lower Deansgate Area

To examine the relationship between floor-area and trip-generation we looked at data for the 103 firms. These were used to make a graphical plot in which the ordinate values were the weekly goods vehicle trips per 1000 square feet. The distribution obtained seemed susceptible of more fruitful treatment if plotted logarithmically and this was done. Simple linear regression and correlation calculations were then made with the following results:

> Mean floor-area: 2050 square feet (antilog 3·3116)
> Mean number of trips per 1000 square feet: 11·5

The standard errors of the logarithms of floor-area and trips per 1000 square feet were 0·339 and 0·412 respectively. The two variables had a correlation of −0·68, while the regression equations were

$$x = -0.53y + 3.88$$
$$y = -0.82x + 3.79$$

Unfortunately the errors of measurement in x and y are not independent, since the values of y have been obtained by dividing the number of trips t by floor-area x, and so errors in x are incorporated in the errors in y. Accordingly we did another analysis relating to x. The mean weekly number of trips was 23·39. In this case the correlation between log t and log x was lower, at 0·24, with a standard error of 0·0915. This is reasonably significant. The regression equations were

$$\log_{10}x = 0.24 \log_{10}t + 2.99$$
$$\text{and} \quad \log_{10}t = 0.25 \log_{10}x + 0.55$$

The last equation can be written as

$$t = 3.55x^{0.25}$$

which provides the best estimate of trips given a knowledge only of floor space. We may note that trips per unit floor-space would be

$$\frac{t}{x} = 3 \cdot 55x^{-0 \cdot 75}$$

which may be compared with the statistically less satisfactory estimate based on the earlier regression equation of

$$y = \frac{t}{x} = 6 \cdot 12x^{-0 \cdot 82}.$$

In either case, trips per unit floor-space are lower for the larger units than for the smaller ones.

Note. The analysis for this appendix was undertaken by Mr J. B. McLoughlin.

Urban Land Values in Classical Economics

Classical economists were concerned more with agricultural land than with urban land. As a factor of production it was combinable with labour in varying proportions. Even today the simplest expositions of marginal analysis rely upon the Ricardian assumptions that all land is identical, and that it can be brought into use in infinitesimally small increments. An important advance, in which the location of the land was considered, was made by J. H. von Thünen in 1826.[1] When economists turned to study urban land they simplified the problems almost out of existence, until Marshall wrote his *Principles of Economics*.[2] This contains a great deal of fundamental observation and thought, which have too long been rather neglected, especially in Marshall's own country. He explains why 'shops which deal in expensive and choice objects tend to congregate together; and those which supply ordinary domestic needs do not'.[3] His very next sentence reads, 'Every cheapening of the means of communications, every new facility for the free interchange of ideas between distant places alters the action of the forces which tend to localize industries.' Then he moves to consider international freights and urban–rural flows. Communication within a town has no mention.

Much later in his book Marshall discusses land values and marginal costs. It is worth summarising his argument.[4] He considers two producers who 'have equal facilities in all respects, except that one has a more convenient situation than the other, and can buy or sell in the same markets with less cost of carriage'. Nearness to 'a labour market specially adapted to his trade . . . can be translated in like manner into money values. When this is done, and all are added together we have the money value of the advantages of situation which the first business has over the second: and this becomes its special *situation value*, if the second has no situation value and its site is reckoned merely at agricultural value!'

The situation value is thus exclusive of the agricultural value of the site. It is a measure of the worth of locational advantages. Marshall then defined site value 'of any piece of building land' as 'that which it would have if cleared of buildings and sold in a free market'. It followed that site value was the sum of special situation value and agricultural value.

After noting 'that the greater part of situation value is public value', resulting from the action of men other than its owners, he went on to instance examples where this was not so. Coming to the case of a man who lays out a neighbourhood for development, he pointed out that the 'collective value' thus created by him 'is of the nature of public value; and it is dependent, for the greater part, on that dormant public value, which the site as a whole derived from the growth of a prosperous town in its neighbourhood. But that share of it which arises from his forethought, constructive faculty and outlay, is to be regarded as the reward of business enter-prise, rather than as the appropriation of public value by a private person.'

Turning to the determinants of the value at which land can be sold, and of the ground-rent at which it can be let, Marshall defined the former as the actuarial discounted value 'of all the net incomes which it is likely to afford' after taking account of expenses and 'its capabilities of development'. He asserted that the annual ground-rent, fixed for the duration of the lease, was such that the discounted payment stream tended to equal the present capital value of the land, adjusted for the obligation to hand over the land complete with buildings on termination of the lease, and for any inconvenience due to restrictions on the use of the land.

At this stage Marshall applied his marginal analysis. If a site has no scarcity value, the amount of capital per square foot that, when used for building, will maximise returns from the site will vary with the purpose for which the building is wanted. 'But when the site has a scarcity value, it is worth while to go on applying capital beyond this maximum rather than pay the extra cost of land required for extending the site.' He applied the phrase *the margin of building* to 'that accommodation which it is only just worth while to get from a given site, and which would not be got from it if land were less scarce'.

Assuming 'that the competition for land for various uses will cause building in each locality and for each use to be carried up to that margin, at which it is no longer profitable to apply any more capital to the same site', Marshall reminded us that site value should not be regarded as governing marginal costs. Rather was it that when expenses of production rose 'so high that people were willing to pay a high value for additional land in order to avoid the inconvenience and expense of crowding their work on to a narrow site. These causes govern site value. . . .'

He went on to explain why shops in some localities could charge high prices and so fetch high rents. Sometimes a 'situation becomes more valuable for purposes other than shopkeeping'. Many shopkeepers will move out. Those remaining may be able to charge higher prices, reflecting the higher ground-rents.

Except for a valuable appendix on the incidence of local rates, this effectively ends Marshall's analysis. In it are the germs of a modern theory. Marshall did not direct his thoughts to urban land values when writing of location, and his analysis of land values is accordingly incomplete; but so are most of the more recent theories.[5]

The essential point is that Marshall considers the density of development of a site to depend upon the marginal costs of additional development and the marginal returns derivable from its occupation. These latter reflect the situation value, and stem from the convenience, or advantages, of the location to a potential user, when he compares one site with another. Transport can affect the comparison.

The Division of a Town into Zones

The census of population divides British towns into enumeration districts, each containing approximately 300 private households, and defined partly with reference to local-government boundaries (which are often of historical origin and of little other significance) and partly with an eye on the convenience of the enumerator. There is clearly an argument for building our zones out of whole enumeration districts, and because these are quite small it is often possible to do so in a way that does not violate considerations of the kind mentioned below. Two disadvantages are that the enumeration districts of one census often differ from those of the next census, and that information about shops, traffic and so on may be available only for areas bearing little relationship to them.

Chiefly in an attempt to secure stability of the boundaries over time, partly to avoid the accusation of being prejudiced in favour of one set of boundaries rather than another, and partly to avoid the troublesome task of defining more 'real' boundaries, there is now a strong movement in favour of collecting and publishing data on a grid-square basis. The main trouble here is that unless the squares are very small (when publication may involve breach of confidence) they may be too large to provide good fits with more meaningful zones.

For the purpose of model building, the greater the number of characteristics that are reasonably homogeneous over the zone, the easier the subsequent analysis is likely to be. But attempts to define zonal boundaries on this basis will almost immediately raise two problems. Is it more important for a zone to contain a more or less constant X or a more or less constant Y? Should boundaries run down the middle of a street, or should they perhaps run through backgardens and buildings?

There is no single answer to these questions. One line of attack may be to wander around an area, getting a feel for it, and defining the boundaries by locating the points where some kind of transition is most apparent: but the answer may well depend on the time of the day, as well as on many subjective considerations. Some boundaries are obvious to anybody, but others have no single right place. There is a no-man's-land in which the frontier is known to exist, but its precise location cannot be logically defined, any more than old age can be said to begin on one's fiftieth or sixtieth birthday.

It may well be that the model-builder should compile a list of meaningful, easily observed and fairly static attributes to which particular importance may be attached. One could, for example, suggest that every zone should have one major land-use occupying at least half of its area; that the range of rateable values or ground-rents should not exceed a certain amount; that streets of houses with no front gardens should not be in the same zone as other streets; and so on. In this way some degree of homogeneity may arise, and this may be useful. The compilation of the list and the setting of priorities within it will clearly be influenced by both the interests and the prejudices of the model-builder.

Purely statistical techniques, defining zones according to the value of a single statistic or to the characteristics of a set, may be less obviously subjective, and in many respects preferable.

In the end the critical questions may be 'Does it look right?' and 'Does it look wrong?' How, after all, would one divide a hundred men into seven groups if one's purpose were to examine the interactions of groups? For the town, geographical contiguity helps: but a probably insoluble problem remains. What matters, and what every model-builder should consider, is that the description of a zone should not be simply in terms of averages, and that eventually the sensitivity of the model to changes in zonal boundaries should be examined.

There are obvious advantages if the study of one town can to some extent be used in another. Urban research is too costly for us to be indifferent to the prospect of transferability, but there are many obstacles to it. One is the lack of uniformity in our definitions of zones. To some extent this could be reduced by ensuring that every zone was of the same size, or of the same population, or contained precisely one school. Within a given study this procedure can be useful, but the constraint so imposed may be a positive hindrance to another study.

A different approach is to note that no zone is complete in itself, and that the various traffics have to be considered. This can be done more systematically if all zones have precisely the same number of neighbouring zones. If, for example, every zone, whatever its shape or size, has exactly six neighbours, and no point is contiguous to more than three zones, then conceptually every town can be thought of as an array of regular hexagons. If we know the characteristics of each zone, including its size and shape (or ratio of perimeter to area, or some related statistic), then we can compare one town with another by looking, first, at the zonal characteristics. In some cases they may be sufficiently similar for us to have some faith in the transference of results. The traffic linkages can be the six flows across the hexagonal boundaries.

In Figure A6.1 we have taken a simplified version of the main road structure of part of central Exeter, and devised a set of zones. Each has precisely six neighbouring zones. In devising them we have been concerned with the locations of the nodes rather than with the paths of the boundaries. Zone 4 is nothing more than a busy road intersection. Zone 5 is High Street. Zone 11 is chiefly the cathedral close, while zone 17 is the university campus.

It is now possible to describe Exeter fairly precisely by listing the various characteristics of each zone. Two such characteristics could be the radial distance and bearing of the centre of the zone from the centre of the city. Other towns can be similarly described. It is unlikely that many would have marked similarities to the whole of Exeter, but we may note two important points. One is that the contiguity of the High Street and the cathedral close is a common feature of English towns, and that possibly the patterns in zones 5 and 11 and their neighbouring zones may be fairly similar in several cities. The second point is that any grid of hexagons may be transformed into a coarser grid by combining the zones into groups of seven, as indicated by the heavy lines in the diagrams. Now the coarse zone containing the cathedral may reasonably be called the central area. The coarse zone containing the university is otherwise chiefly residential, and includes the zones in which a large proportion of the inhabitants are students or staff. At this stage of aggregation the likelihood of fruitful comparison with other towns seems to increase.

Apart from providing a form of transformation that allows us mathematically to 'map' one town onto another, this idea may also

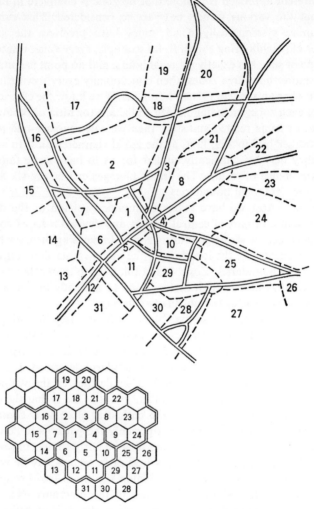

Figure A6.1. Illustrative division of Exeter in hexagons

encourage theorists to develop a corpus of theorems about conceptual hexagons with certain characteristics and linkages, thereby enriching the study of real towns. We may move from studies of towns to a study of towns.

One could, of course, have conceptual triangles or squares instead of hexagons. Hexagons have been chosen because they provide the maximum number of linkages that is compatible with a regular geometry. They are flexible enough to accommodate concentric patterns as a special case.

There is hardly need to point out that such a scheme can be used for both artificial and real models. One of its advantages is that if enough work is done on artificial models built on this (or some other) standard scheme, then one may find certain patterns emerging. Because every zone has the same number of neighbours, any existing patterns will be more readily noticed and more easily classified. Perhaps one will find that over quite a wide range of urban descriptions, variation of certain behavioural parameters or assumptions has negligible long-term effect. In such a case, those whose concern is to test hypotheses or to measure parameters may consider it fruitful to devote their time to testing or measuring in more critical fields. This possibility does not, of course, depend on the use of hexagonal zones: but if many models were based on such a scheme, then the very fact that, topologically, the towns would be similar, and could all be mapped into each other, should facilitate the integration of our studies.

An Outline for an Urban Model

These notes outline some first thoughts on a computer model for a town. As it stands it is artificial, but it involves quantities that are measurable, and the behavioural assumptions are, for the most part, testable. It has weaknesses, but no single assumption is essential, and there is no reason why, as our knowledge and techniques improve, the various parts of the model should not be improved. It can become a model for a real, specific town.

Even as it stands, however, it is of some use. If we set the model working, and then introduce some restraint, such as a land-use regulation or a development tax, or if we impose some public-authority development or build a road, then we can see the full consequences, in our model town, of the action. Since we are not yet in the position to experiment with real towns, the lessons to be learned from models may at least be worth considering: and the more realistic our models can be made, the more useful they should be.

In this model we use a set of matrices to describe a town at a given moment, in terms of its land-uses, the intensities of development and rents. We also introduce transport linkages.

At the beginning of every year certain leases fall in, and the property is redeveloped or left as it is according to a set of behavioural rules. These take account of building costs, expected rents and other factors. One of these depends on transport.

Just as the distribution of land-use affects transport requirements and rental movements, so these in turn affect land-use and the intensity of development. Similarly, the extent and kind of redevelopment affects building costs. Failure to let at an adequate rent implies the onset of physical decay, which in turn affects the rent obtainable for that and surrounding property.

These feed-backs are introduced into the second part of the model, which concerns a whole town. The first part looks at a single zone, in order to present the basic mechanism.

Throughout this account the approach is mechanically deterministic. It would be better, especially at certain indicated points, to introduce probability distributions. Eventually this will have to be done. Here our emphasis is on a causal chain, in an attempt to provide a fairly simple explanation, which can later be modified.

Before presenting the model we may remark upon another of its uses. In redeveloping an existing town, or planning a new one, one should naturally examine the consequences of one's actions. One must also consider the demands upon resources. We have already indicated briefly how our model may take account of the problems. But we must also consider whether the town operates efficiently—whether, for example, there is, as the result of one design (or lack of it), excessive traffic-generation. Our model can be used for this purpose. It can also be used to indicate to what extent alternative possible actions now effectively preserve land-use or other choices for posterity. There is a case, when planning, for paying more attention to this than we do.

Part 1. A Single Zone. Descriptive Matrices

1. First we consider a single *zone*, divided into *plots*. Each plot has an associated land-use (which may be no use), and the development upon it (measured as a ratio of floor-space to plot-area) lies within a certain intensity range. We can consequently compile a matrix, denoted briefly A^t, descriptive of the situation at a specified moment. Its elements will indicate the number of plots with a given land-use and development intensity.

2. There will be a similar matrix for any moment. We define our time interval to be a *year*, which need not be a calendar year: it may be longer or shorter. The typical element of the land-use intensity matrix for year $t + 1$ will be

$$a_{ij}^{t+1}$$

3. We suppose that all property is leased. As an initial simplification we suppose that all leases are of the same length, but have varying dates of expiry; that no property comes onto the market for development except when a lease expires; that when a lease expires the recent leaseholder has to compete with others if he wishes

to renew his lease. We summarise the numbers of plots of various kinds whose leases expire *at the commencement of year t* by a matrix L^t, whose elements l^t_{ij} indicate numbers of properties of intensity i and type j.

4. One of the factors determining decisions about development will be levels of rent. These will depend upon land-use and intensity of development, as well as upon other factors. We denote the levels of rents obtained for properties leased in period t by values of r^t_{ij}, which are elements of the matrix R^t. This assumes that in each period at least one lease is let in each category. Later we specify a rule for determining a notional r_{ij} if no lease is let.

5. We denote by $'\bar{R}^t$ the matrix of rents which developers expect in period t to get from leases let in period t, and by $'\bar{R}^{t+1}$ what they expect in period t to get from leases of property withdrawn from the market for a year for redevelopment and let on new leases in period $t + 1$. The elements in this second matrix denoted by $'\bar{r}^{t+1}_{ij}$, refer to the land-use and intensity after development.

6. Construction or conversion costs for operations carried out in period t depend on the initial land-use and intensity and the final land-use and intensity. They can be denoted by the elements c^t_{ijkl} (where the land use intensity changes from ij to kl) of the matrix.

7. We use the matrices D^t and E^t to indicate, respectively, the demands at the commencement of period t, at existing rent structures, for new leases of various land-use intensities, and the number of such leases not taken up (i.e. properties left empty) by the end of the period.

8. Transport will be brought into the model when we consider a town consisting of several zones. So will decay.

Behavioural Relationships

9. In the following paragraphs we indicate various relationships between the entries in these matrices. Some of these relationships involve exogenous factors. At this stage we make no attempt to justify the relationships, but we shall later have to consider the extent to which they are realistic and suggest possibly more realistic modification. Eventually they must be tested empirically.

10. When ij leases fall vacant, the owners can leave them unchanged and expect to get a rent $'\bar{r}_{ij}$ for n years. Alternatively they can withdraw them for a year, thus losing a year's rent, spend an amount

c_{ijkl} converting them to kl, and then expect a rent of $^t\bar{r}^t$ for a rent of $n-1$ years.

As a very simple set of rules for deciding what happens we may adopt the following.

11. The expected rent $^t\bar{r}^t_{ij}$ at which a new lease can be let, without any change in land-use intensity, is based on the actual rents at which similar leases have been let in that zone in recent periods. If no such leases have been let in that zone, then evidence is drawn in from other zones, in a way to be described in the multi-zone model. If no such leases have been let anywhere, then an estimate is made according to a rule to be described later.

12. As a specific rule one may suppose that, according to whether there are empty properties of that land-use intensity (either in the zone concerned, or perhaps, in neighbouring zones), then

if $\quad e^{t-1}_{ij} = 0, \quad {}^t\bar{r}^t_{ij} = r^{t-1}_{ij} + (r^{t-1}_{ij} - r^{t-2}_{ij})$

if $\quad e^{t-1}_{ij} > 0, \quad {}^t\bar{r}^t_{ij} = r^{t-1}_{ij} + L[(r^{t-1}_{ij} - r^{t-2}_{ij}, 0)]$

where $L[x,y]$ indicates the lower of the values x,y.

These rules specify that if there are no empty properties the current expectation of rents obtainable in the period now beginning will continue the rent revealed by the change in rents in the last period. If, however, there are empty properties, the expected rent is the most recently determined actual rent or less.

13. Similarly we may suggest that

if $\quad e^{t-1}_{ij} = 0, \quad {}^t\bar{r}^{t+1}_{ij} = r^{t-1}_{ij} + 2(r^{t-1}_{ij} - r^{t-2}_{ij})$

if $\quad e^{t-1}_{ij} > 0, \quad {}^t\bar{r}^{t+1}_{ij} = r^{t-1}_{ij} + 2L[(r^{t-1}_{ij} - r^{t-2}_{ij}, 0)]$

14. Against the expected rental incomes have to be set construction or conversion costs. These, specified by the matrix C, can take account of several factors. If a particular kind of conversion or intensification is not allowed—such as when planning policy forbids a particular kind of land-use change—then we can take account of it by putting the relevant costs at infinity. In a complete model, in which urban development is set in the context of a national economy, the matrix C can have values depending on the rate of interest and the demand for and supply of building resources. This means that in the second part of the model the level of activity generated by the

model will have to be one of the factors determining the matrix of costs.

15. Comparison of all possible gains in expected rental income and the related costs will reveal a (not necessarily unique) most profitable course of action.

16. In a later version of the model we may attach probabilities to various rental incomes, and rank the expected gains not only in terms of magnitude but also in terms of probability.

17. Until we introduce the modification in paragraph 16, when we shall be able to specify a variety of development decisions in a specified land-use intensity situation, we suppose that all developers with a given land-use intensity in our zone reach the same decision, by selecting (according to 15) the most profitable course of action. If there is more than one 'most profitable' course, then they are all followed equally.

18. The supply of vacant leases in period t will consist of those leases just surrendered, which are not going to be developed, plus those that were redeveloped in the previous period, plus those remaining empty from earlier periods. For brevity we may denote this supply by $S^t = [s_{ij}^t]$.

19. The numbers of leases taken up, and the rents settled, will depend upon the demands, as well as on S^t. For any land-use the various intensities are to some extent competitive with each other. Once we extend the model to include several zones, then the competition from the other zones has also to be taken into account.

20. In specifying a decision rule here, we have to keep in mind that empirical work may well suggest a different one. For the time being the following approach does not appear to be too implausible. As an alternative approach, which would in some respects be superior we could apply probability concepts.

21. We suppose that within a specified land-use a different intensity of development also means a different standard; and that people are prepared to pay higher rents per square foot of floor-space in the higher standard buildings. In the case of offices, standards may rise with intensity, while for dwellings the reverse may be true.

22. We also suppose that tenants set a maximum to the difference they are prepared to see between the rent per square foot for accommodation of one standard and that of the next best standard. Developers set a minimum to this difference.

Denoting the rents per square foot of accommodation of intensity i (land-use j being understood) by P_i, and the ratio

$$\frac{P_{i+1}}{P_i}$$

by σ_i then (in the case where rents per square foot rise with intensity) the above assumption can be expressed as

$$\sigma_i^{\max} \geqslant \sigma_i \geqslant \sigma_i^{\min}$$

23. The demand for new tenancies of leases of a specified land-use will consist of a basic demand, modified by consideration of rent. We shall consider the determinants of the basic demand shortly. For the moment we take it for granted and denote it by Δ_i. The actual demand denoted by D_i' may be written as

$$D_i' = \Delta_i(1 + \sum \alpha_{iz}P_z)$$

where z ranges over all possible intensities, and the α's indicate the dependence of the level of demand for leases of intensity i upon the rents charged for leases at all intensities in the same land-use. For any i,

$$\alpha_{iz} \geqslant 0 \quad \text{for} \quad z \neq i, \qquad \alpha_{iz} \leqslant 0 \quad \text{for} \quad z = i$$

24. Let the supply of floor-area—as opposed to leases—at intensity i be S_i'

write
$$P_1 = P_0\sigma_0^{\max}$$
$$P_2 = P_1\sigma_1^{\max} \quad \text{etc.}$$

The vector $[P_i]$ now represents a scheme of rents that, for any given P_0, is the one most favourable to the owners of property of intensity 0, within the constraint imposed by the tenants' ideas of maximum differentials.

With these values of P_i, express D_0' in terms of P_0. This gives us a demand schedule for leases of intensity 0 in terms of rents of such leases. There is a fixed supply S_0'. We also stipulate a minimum rent below which owners of such property would prefer to see it empty.

Choose a value of D_0' equal to S_0' and evaluate P_0. If this is beneath the minimum, then set the rent at its minimum acceptable value, thus determining the number of properties left empty, as well as the actual rent per square foot.

If the rent is equal to or above the minimum, then no properties of this intensity are left empty, and the actual rent is determined.

Multiplication of this rent by σ_0^{min} determines the lowest acceptable rent for property of intensity 1.

The vector

$$[P_0, P_1, P_1, \sigma_1^{max}, \qquad P_1 \sigma_1^{max} \sigma_2^{max} \dots]$$

s now the one most favourable to owners of property of intensity 1, given the value of P_0.

We now express the demand for property of intensity 1 in terms of P_1. Equating it to the supply we consider whether P_1 is above its minimum acceptable value. If it is not, then there are empty properties. If it is, then we also consider if it is below its acceptable maximum, based on the differential. If it is, then the actual rent is that which equates demand to supply. If it is not, then we fractionally increase Δ_0, and make a corresponding reduction in Δ_1, as the demand curves shift, before starting the calculations again.

Proceeding in this way we obtain the actual levels of the rent per square foot, and the numbers of empty properties, at every level of intensity. Several iterations may be necessary before the various constraints are all met. If one can alight on reasonably realistic values for the α_{iz} and σ, which should be possible with adequate market investigations, then the number of iterations should be reduced.

25. According to the intensity factors, the rents per square foot determined in 24 can be converted into actual plot rents, r_{ij}.

26. The foregoing paragraphs determine the development during year t, the actual rents charged, and the number of empty properties. Along with the number of leases falling vacant at the beginning of year $t + 1$ (which is defined by the number of leases let n years previously), these data specify the matrices for the next year, and the calculations continue.

27. We have yet to tie up certain loose ends. These are:

(i) the determination of r_{ij} if no lease of kind ij is let (paragraph 4);

(ii) the determination of $^t\bar{r}_{ij}^t$ in similar circumstances (paragraph 11).

Clearly both of these problems are more easily solved when there are other zones. In a single-zone model we have to adopt some device such as that of estimating these values from the known values for similar, rather than identical, land-use intensities.

28. We also have to specify the determinants of the basic demand, Δ. In a single-zone model these can be taken as exogenous. In a multi-zone model they depend on inter-zonal comparisons, transport, and other matters.

Part II. Many Zones

29. Each zone will be characterised by its matrices as defined for the single zone.

30. Over each boundary there will be flows of traffic. These may include vehicles, pedestrians, telephone calls, inter-zonal activity (such as football matches). They can be specified numerically or attributively. The specification of any one traffic may be a vector whose elements are associated with different times of the day, week or year.

31. There will be related vectors describing flows from one zone to a non-contiguous zone.

32. Each zone will have a set of parameters, indicating its 'attractiveness' to different kinds of users. They will depend upon such factors as the extent of decay, land-use, land-use in neighbouring zones, and time taken to reach zones of certain characteristics (e.g. nearest largely residential zone or group of these, nearest zone with more than x per cent of plots devoted to high density office buildings, etc.). Here the 'time' of the more remote zones may be recorded simply as in excess of a certain limit.

33. These parameters influence demand schedules, and lead to prospective and actual tenants comparing not only different intensities, but also different locations.

34. A change in land-use leads to changes in traffic-generation, and so on all matters affected by this, including the parameters of paragraph 32.

35. The rate of decay of buildings in a zone will depend on the extent of empty property and the duration of its emptiness, on changes in levels of rents, on owner's expectations and on costs.

36. The above notes indicate the broad lines along which the model was started in September 1967 in the Centre for Urban and Regional Research at Manchester University with a grant from the Social Science Research Council. A more up-to-date account is available from the Centre.

Future Urban Land Requirements

According to R. H. Best and J. T. Coppock[1] there were 2·5 million acres of land devoted to urban use in the urban areas of England and Wales in 1951. There were also 1·1 million acres devoted to 'urban uses' (such as roads) outside urban areas.

If the population increases by 48 per cent between 1951 and 2001, and there is a *pro rata* increase in land needs, then the total area devoted to urban uses will rise from 3·6 million acres to 5·3 million acres.

Alternative and more realistic assumptions increase this estimate.

If the projected population increase is housed at thirty persons per acre, and total urban land requirements are put at double the housing acreage, then 1·4 million acres will be required. If, in addition, about 6 million houses are replaced between 1951 and 2001 at these new densities, then probably another 0·6 million acres will be needed. This total of 2 million acres reflects only the needs that will arise within urban areas. If the urban uses outside urban areas grow in the same proportion, then the total need will be about 2·9 million acres more than now, representing a total acreage of 6·5 million.

This calculation ignores additional requirements, which may arise from expected decreases in household sizes, increased life expectancy and other factors. Between them these could easily add another 0·5 million acres to the total needs by 2001.

Local Authorities
and Housing Improvements

(Most of this appendix is based on a document prepared by the Ministry of Housing for a private conference on urban renewal.) The existing (mid-1967) powers of local authorities in England and Wales for dealing with housing improvements are described briefly in this appendix. It concludes with a summary of proposals contained in the White Paper *Old Houses into New Homes* (Cmnd 3602) published in April 1968.

The Housing Act of 1957 enables authorities to deal with dwellings unfit for human habitation. The Housing (Financial Provisions) Act, 1958 enables (but does not require) authorities to make grants to private owners for the improvement or conversion of their houses to a fairly high standard. It also enables the Exchequer to make grants towards the cost of improving and converting houses owned by local authorities or by housing associations. The other important provision is that authorities who have acquired houses for future demolition may receive Exchequer grants towards the cost of patching them if they cannot reasonably be demolished immediately.

In 1959 the House Purchase and Housing Act was passed. Unlike the permissive Acts just mentioned, this compels housing authorities to pay a standard grant to owners towards the cost of bringing the provision of certain basic amenities up to standard. It is concerned with the state of repair to only a very limited extent. Local authorities carrying out similar improvements to their own houses may obtain Exchequer grants.

Houses in multiple occupation were the subject of the 1961 Housing Act, which gave local authorities power to apply certain rules of management and to insist on work necessary if certain standards were to be reached. The power to compel private owners to improve their dwellings, introduced in the 1961 Act for those in multiple occupation, was extended to all privately owned dwellings by the Housing Act, 1964.

In 1967 the Housing Subsidies Act provided that housing associations buying or modernising houses by arrangement with local authorities could receive subsidies based on the combined costs of acquisition, conversion and improvement.

Local authorities have a statutory duty to deal, by reconditioning or clearance, with houses in their district found to be unfit for habitation. Unfit houses can be dealt with individually or collectively by clearance area. Authorities can deal with an area of unfit houses by making a clearance order requiring owners to demolish, but leaving the land with the owners; or by acquiring the houses, by agreement or compulsorily, and themselves carrying out demolition. Authorities may also acquire adjoining property to provide a satisfactory area for redevelopment. The redevelopment of the cleared area is within the control of local authorities, whether they carry this out themselves or sell the land to private developers.

The standard by which the fitness of a house is judged is not precisely defined, but is statutorily related to repair, stability, freedom from damp, natural lighting, ventilation, water supply, drainage and sanitary conveniences and arrangements for storing, preparing and cooking food and for the disposal of waste water. A house may be condemned only if it is so far defective in one or more of these items as to be not reasonably suitable for occupation.

A clearance or compulsory purchase order is subject to confirmation by the minister. All owners have a right to object, and, if objections are made, a public local inquiry is held by one of the minister's inspectors before a decision is reached on the order.

The powers of compulsory purchase or improvement have associated principles of compensation. In slum-clearance the compensation code assumes that the public should not have to pay for houses that have been condemned as unfit to live in, and the compensation is normally limited to the value of the site cleared of buildings and ready for development. This rule was first introduced in 1919, and the basic principle has been upheld by every Government since then, although some exceptions have been introduced. It has been regarded as fundamental to an effective slum-clearance programme, various earlier attempts having failed largely because of the financial obstacles.

When the slum-clearance drive was resumed in 1956, after the wartime suspension, provision was made for supplementary payments to owner-occupiers who bought their houses between 1 September 1939 and 12 December 1955, while slum-clearance was in abeyance, to bring their compensation up to the market value of their houses as if they had not been found unfit. This provision was due to expire on 13 December 1965, but was continued by the Housing (Slum Clearance Compensation) Act, 1965, for those qualifying owner-occupiers who have not had fifteen years' possession of their houses at the date the order is made.

Alternatively, where, despite their inherent defects, unfit houses have been well maintained, both owners and tenants can qualify for additional payments. For an owner-occupied house the amount is at least four times, and in any other case at least twice, the rateable value of the house. If, however, the authorities are satisfied that a greater sum has been spent on maintenance in the preceding five years, the payment may equal the actual expenditure less one and a quarter times the rateable value.

To deal with the problem of very small sites, which may be virtually worthless, it is provided that no owner-occupier shall receive less than the gross value of the house. Owner-occupiers of condemned houses have a right to apply to the county court for the discharge or modification of any outstanding mortgage liability.

People who run a business from an unfit house in which their interest is greater than a tenancy for a year are entitled to the full market value of their interest, subject to certain conditions being satisfied.

Local authorities have discretionary powers to pay removal expenses incurred by people displaced by slum-clearance. They can pay an allowance towards trade losses sustained by owners of property included in slum-clearance orders who do not qualify for the statutory business-occupiers' supplement, for example, to tenants whose interest is for a year or less. Authorities may also make an allowance to small shopkeepers in the locality who, although their properties are not being acquired, will suffer business losses due to the clearance action.

The word 'improvements' is used in a narrowly defined technical sense. It does not include ordinary repairs or the renewal of obsolete or worn-out installations and equipment, for which (up to the time of writing, in mid-1967) there are no grants. The first objective is to provide amenities in houses that are structurally sound. The second is to increase the number of dwellings by converting older houses that are too large for the modern family into two or more flats, or by bringing other buildings into housing use. Grants are paid by local authorities to owners to encourage conversions and improvements, and to meet half the cost of improvements within certain maxima. Three-quarters of the grant paid by the local authority is recovered from the Exchequer. There are two types of grant. All grants must be approved before works are started and are payable to freeholders or leaseholders with at least fifteen years of the lease to run or, in the case of ground lessees, if there are five years of the lease to run. After improvement with the aid of a grant there are certain conditions that are required to be observed for a period of three years.

Discretionary grants were introduced in 1949 and are payable at the discretion of a local authority for improvements and conversions to a relatively high level of repair and amenity. This is intended to give the sort of standard one would normally expect to find in a modern house, when allowance is made for age and limitations in design layout and construction. To get a discretionary grant a dwelling must be such that it will achieve the Twelve Point Standard after improvement or conversion. This standard is as follows:

1. The house must be in a good state of repair and substantially free from damp.
2. Each room must be properly lighted and ventilated.
3. An adequate supply of wholesome water must be laid on in the dwelling.
4. Efficient and adequate means of supplying hot water for domestic purposes must be provided.
5. It must have an internal water closet, if practicable, otherwise a readily accessible outside water closet.
6. It must have a fixed bath or shower in a bathroom.
7. A sink, or sinks, and with suitable arrangements for the disposal of waste water must be provided.
8. It must have a proper drainage system.
9. Each room must be provided with adequate points for gas or electric lighting (where reasonably available).
10. There must be adequate facilities for heating.
11. Satisfactory facilities for storing, preparing and cooking food must be available.

12. There must be proper provision for storing fuel where necessary.

In addition the local authority must also be satisfied that a house is likely to have a useful life of thirty years in normal cases, or exceptionally between fifteen and thirty years. A local authority may pay up to one-half the estimated cost of works up to a maximum grant of £400 per house improved or per flat provided by conversion. However, where flats are produced by conversion of a house of three or more storeys, the upper limit of the grant is £500 per flat.

Standard grants were introduced in 1959 to encourage the provision of the basic amenities of bath, wash-hand basin, hot and cold water supply, inside water closet and food store in houses that lack them. Local authorities are obliged to pay standard grants provided certain statutory conditions are fulfilled. One of these conditions is that the house concerned must have been built before 1945, and another is that it will be fit to live in for at least fifteen years. The grant is half the cost of improvements, subject to a maximum obtained by adding together the amounts specified for the missing amenities. These are as follows:

1. a fixed bath or shower	£25
2. wash-hand basin	£5
3. (a) a hot and cold water supply at a fixed bath or shower	£35
(b) a hot and cold water supply at a wash-hand basin	£15
(c) a hot and cold water supply at a sink	£25
4. an inside water closet	£40
5. a satisfactory food store	£10
	£155

A grant higher than the normal maximum is payable in cases where the improvement necessarily involves such major work as building on extensions, supplying piped water for the first time or providing septic-tank drainage: in such cases the maximum is £350. After improvement, a house must normally have all five of the basic amenities, but in certain cases a grant may be payable where a house will achieve a reduced standard, consisting of at least the amenities described at 3 (c), 4 and 5 above.

Local authorities can obtain Exchequer contributions for the improvement of their own houses on a similar basis to those paid for private owners. Housing associations can obtain grants on the same basis as private owners. As an alternative they can make arrangements with a local authority to receive Exchequer contributions in the same way as the authority. A further alternative has been given in the Housing Subsidies Act. A housing association can now make arrangements with a local authority to receive an Exchequer subsidy based on the costs of acquiring properties and converting or improving them. The maximum combined cost of acquisition and works taken into account for this purpose is £2000 a dwelling, aggregated for the number of dwellings produced for each conversion.

In 1964 local authorities were given powers to require the provision of the basic amenities in fit dwellings occupied by tenants. Local authorities are now required to inspect their districts with a view to defining areas suitable for compulsory improvement. Having declared an improvement area, a local authority may compel landlords to install the five basic amenities in their houses. Outside these areas, tenants of individual houses can ask local authorities to force their landlords to bring them up to a similar standard, and local authorities also have powers to compel the improvement of tenement blocks.

Local authorities are advised to secure as much voluntary improvement as possible, but, where this is not forthcoming, improvement notices may be enforced by the council, who have the power to carry out necessary works and recover costs. The procedure for compulsory improvement is complex. There are, however, three phases.

1. After inspecting its district a local authority may declare an improvement area and publish notices in the local Press.

2. Notices explaining the council's proposals are served on persons with an interest in the properties, and a meeting fixed to discuss the proposals.

3. In the absence of voluntary undertakings the council may then proceed to serve notices requiring the works to be done.

The procedure provides for the tenants' consent to be received and gives owners rights of appeal to the county court. Local authorities requiring works under these powers have a duty to offer loans to owners to assist with their share of the costs. Persons with an interest in properties affected by compulsory improvement may also require the council to purchase their interest.

Under the Housing Acts a local authority's powers to enforce repairs are limited to unfit houses. If these powers are involved, the house must be made fit, but the standard required is sufficient only to raise the property out of the demolition class. The local authority must be satisfied that the necessary repairs are capable of being carried out at a reasonable expense. A landlord can appeal to the county court against the notice served on him by the local authority.

Local authorities have powers under the Public Health Acts to deal with statutory nuisances. These powers are used in relation to houses to enforce specific repairs, not necessarily involving unfitness. But the extent of the repairs is confined merely to abating the nuisance that gave rise to the local authority's action.

Finally we must say a word about multiple occupation. The Housing Act dealing with it refers to 'houses let in lodgings or occupied by members of more than one family'. Before 1954, control of multi-occupied houses was affected by by-laws under Section 6 of the 1936 Housing Act. Owing to increasing concern about conditions in multi-occupied properties towards the end of the 1950s, more comprehensive powers were included in the 1961 Act. Following experience of the working of these powers, some amendments and additions were made in the 1964 Act.

An outline of some of the main points of existing legislation is given below:

1. The Housing Act, 1961, gave authorities power to make management orders. The owner is obliged to abide by a good management code and keep the house clean and its facilities in good order and repair.

2. A local authority can require the owner to rectify disrepair or to put in extra facilities (e.g. for cooking, heating, washing). It is also open to them to make a direction limiting the number of people occupying the property.

3. Local authorities can submit to the minister schemes for registration of multi-occupied houses. Seven such schemes have been confirmed and are now in operation.

4. Completely new powers introduced in the Housing Act, 1964, enable a local authority to make a 'control order' on a house in which it appears that the safety, welfare or health of the occupants needs to be protected. A 'control order' becomes immediately effective, complete control of the house being taken over by the local authority.

After this text had been completed the Government published *Old Houses into New Homes*. Its main proposals are:

1. Local authorities to have the duty, when surveying the condition of houses in their areas, of considering not only the need to provide new houses, but also the need to deal with unsatisfactory areas.

2. Improvement-area provisions of the Housing Act, 1964, to be repealed.

3. Local authorities to be empowered to declare general-improvement areas, without ministerial approval; to assist households in these areas in improving their houses; and to acquire land and buildings in them for improvement of the environment, improvement of houses or clearance.

4. Local authorities to be able to act as owners' agents in improvement matters.

5. Payments of interest only due on loans for the owners' share of improvement and repair costs to be allowed in appropriate cases, the principal being recovered later.

6. Exchequer grant of 50 per cent for environmental improvement, on costs of up to £100 per dwelling, in general-improvement areas.

7. Local authorities' power to compel owners to repair houses to be extended.

8. Normal maximum discretionary grant to be raised from £400 to £1000.

9. Normal maximum conversion grant to be raised from £500 per dwelling to £1200.

10. Certain repairs and replacements to be eligible for improvement grant.

11. Normal total standard improvement grant to be raised from £155 to £200.

12. Ventilated food store to be removed from standard improvement grant 'basic amenities', and sink added.

13. For standard grant, basic amenities need not all be provided at the same time.

14. Grant may be paid on improvement of houses that will not necessarily last fifteen years longer.

15. Improvement grant may be paid, even if the work has begun before grant approved.

16. Local authorities to be able to impose a time limit within which the work must be done.

17. Assistance towards purchase of houses for improvement and

conversion to be payable to local authorities as well as housing associations.

18. Normal maximum cost of acquisition and conversion or improvement eligible for assistance to be £2500 per dwelling obtained.

19. Rents of tenanted houses that reach a required state to be determined under the Rent Act 1965.

20. Local authorities to have power in certain areas to regulate or prevent proposed multiple occupation of houses.

21. Basic amenities may attract a grant, even if not for the exclusive use of one family.

22. Minor improvements to local authorities' powers to regulate existing multiple occupation.

23. Internal arrangement of a house to be included in the criteria of fitness.

24. Supplementary payments for owner-occupied houses subject to future slum-clearance.

25. Tenanted unfit houses to attract payments of four times rateable value if house has been well maintained.

Notes

CHAPTER 1

1. See, for example, Centre d'Information et d'Étude du Credit, *Le Financement du logement en France et à l'étranger* (Paris, 1966); D. V. Donnison, *The Government of Housing* (London, 1967); O.E.C.D., *The Role of Trade Unions in Housing* (1967), which contains a great deal of factual information on housing in several countries; and *The Economic Problems of Housing,* ed. A. A. Nevitt (London, 1967).
2. Ernest W. Burgess, 'The Growth of the City', chapter 2 in Robert E. Park *et al., The City* (Chicago, 1925).
3. F. Engels, *The Condition of the Working Class in England,* translated and edited by W. O. Henderson and W. H. Chaloner (Oxford, 1958; based on the German first edition of 1845) pp. 54–5.
4. Ibid. p. 70.
5. Homer Hoyt, *The Structure and Growth of Residential Neighbourhoods in American Cities* (Washington, 1939). The theory is summarised in several books, including R. U. Ratcliff, *Urban Land Economics* (New York, 1949) pp. 386–403, and R. Barlowe, *Land Resource Economics* (Englewood Cliffs, N.J., 1958) pp. 267–70.
6. For an analysis of this relationship see J. Parry Lewis, *Building Cycles and Britain's Growth* (London, 1965), especially chapters 2, 4 and 5. For useful data on the cotton industry see any edition of G. R. Porter's *The Progress of the Nation* (London, 1836 *et post*) and T. Ellison's *The Cotton Trade of Great Britain* (London, 1886).
7. Phyllis Deane and W. A. Cole, *British Economic Growth 1688–1959* (Cambridge, 1962), especially pp. 5–12 and chapter III.
8. Described very accurately, with diagrams, by Engels, op. cit. pp. 65–70. He comments: 'What a mistake it has been to waste so much capital in this way! If only a little more money had been spent on these houses when they were first built and if only a small amount of repair work had been carried out regularly these houses might have been maintained in a clean, respectable and habitable condition for years' (p. 70).
9. S. D. Simon, *A Century of City Government, Manchester 1838–1938* (London, 1938) p. 284.
10. Ibid. p. 285.
11. See the mimeographed paper *Housing in Twilight Areas* (published

by the Department of Land Economy, University of Cambridge, 1964).
12. S. E. Rasmussen, *Towns and Buildings* (Liverpool, 1951) p. 173.
13. See the official report entitled *The State of our Schools* (Department of Education and Science: H.M.S.O., London, 1965).
14. We should note that in the timber trade this phenomenon is called 'weathering' rather than 'decay', which refers to decomposition by fungi and other micro-organisms. See J. S. Scott, *A Dictionary of Building* (Penguin Reference Book: London, 1964).
15. Alec Clifton-Taylor, *The Pattern of English Building* (London, 1962) p. 78.
16. The 'natural life' of a building is necessarily an idealised concept. Here we use it to denote the lifetime of a building under the rather artificial circumstances in which it is subjected to the ordinary climatic conditions associated with its location, in which there is no expenditure on maintenance and repair, and when it ceases to be occupied because of its disintegration rather than because of any change in the desires of its occupiers. In other words it does not become functionally obsolescent because of any change from the occupiers' point of view, but it eventually ceases to be useful because of its growing state of decay. It is the period that it takes for a building subjected to climatic and other natural forces, but to no repair expenditure, to reach a state of disintegration in which it ceases to be useful.

CHAPTER 3

1. J. M. Beshers, *Urban Social Structure* (Chicago, 1962) pp. 7–8.
2. See, for example, J. Spencer *et al.*, *Stress and Release on an Urban Housing Estate* (London, 1964) p. 287.
3. W. Foote Whyte, 'Street Corner Society', in *Contributions to Urban Sociology,* ed. E. W. Burgess and D. J. Bogue (Chicago, 1963) p. 257.
4. Marshall B. Clinard, *Slums and Community Development* (London, 1966).
5. E. Gittus, 'Conurbations' (M.A. thesis, University of Liverpool, 1960).
6. W. William-Olsson, 'Stockholm, its Structure and Development', in *Geographical Review,* xxx (1940) 420–38.
7. C. R. Shaw and H. D. McKay, *Juvenile Delinquency and Urban Areas* (Chicago, 1942) p. 21; Chombart de Lauwe *et al.*, *Paris et l'agglomeration Parisienne* (Paris, 1952) pp. 44–102.
8. Housing Research and Development Unit (Director F. M. Jones), Liverpool University School of Architecture.
9. For summary see R. Frankenberg, *Communities in Britain* (Pelican Books, 1966) pp. 174–95.
10. C. Vereker, J. B. Mays *et al.*, *Urban Redevelopment and Social Change*

(Liverpool, 1961) pp. 118–19; R. Wilkinson and D. M. Merry, 'A Statistical Analysis of Attitudes to Moving', in *Urban Studies,* II no. 1 (May 1965).

11. C. Rosser and C. Harris, *The Family and Social Change* (London, 1965).
12. I. M. Castle and E. Gittus, 'The Distribution of Social Defects in Liverpool', in *Sociological Review,* NS V (July 1957).
13. Ibid. Also W. Burns, 'Social Malaise and the Environment' (unpublished interim report, City Planning Office, Newcastle upon Tyne, 1965).
14. C. Vereker, J. B. Mays *et al., Urban Redevelopment,* p. 4.
15. Castle and Gittus, in *Sociological Review,* NS V (July 1957).
16. J. Rex and R. Moore, *Race, Community and Conflict: a study of Sparkbrook* (Oxford, 1967).
17. R. D. McKenzie, 'The Scope of Human Ecology', in *Studies in Human Ecology,* ed. G. A. Theodorson (Evanston, Ill., 1961) p. 35.
18. R. Freedman, 'City Migration, Urban Ecology and Social Theory', in *Contributions,* ed. Burgess and Bogue, pp. 197–8.
19. *Contributions,* ed. Burgess and Bogue, p. 592.
20. L. Wirth, 'Classical Human Ecology', in *Studies,* ed. Theodorson, p. 75.
21. Beshers, *Urban Social Structure,* p. 31.

CHAPTER 5

1. There are, of course, exceptions. Perhaps the most notable is Joseph Chamberlain's replacing of squalor by Corporation Street in Birmingham—see Asa Briggs, *Victorian Cities* (London, 1963).
2. In 1831 Manchester's population of 142,000 was double that of thirty years earlier, and six times the estimated population in 1770. Middlesbrough had a population of only 154 in 1831. Ten years later it had 5463. By 1861 it stood at 19,416, and at the end of the century had reached over 90,000.
3. J. Parry Lewis, *Building Cycles and Britain's Growth* (London, 1965), especially ch. 5 and app. 4.
4. Two notable exceptions are P. Cowan, 'The Problem of Growth, Change, and Ageing in Buildings', in *Transactions of the Bartlett Society,* I (1963) and J. F. Q. Switzer, 'The Life of Buildings in an Expanding Economy', in *Chartered Surveyor,* Aug. 1963.
5. See, for example, P. A. Stone, 'The Economics of Building Designs', in *Journal of the Royal Statistical Society,* series A, vol. CXXIII, pt 3 (1960) p. 259, the same author's *Housing, Town Development, Land and Costs* (London, n.d. [?1963]) p. 90, and his subsequent article 'Urban Development and National Resources', in *Urban Studies,* I, no. 2 (Nov. 1964). In the first of these Stone reports on 'an enquiry carried

out by the Building Research Station among nearly 200 firms in the Midland Region. Nearly a quarter (of the factory buildings) were over 57 years old and a third over 42 years old.' More precisely, out of 174 buildings existing at the end of 1956, 39 had been built before 1900 and 62 before 1915. 'Casual observation would suggest that this pattern is typical for other classes of buildings.' This inquiry, which was conducted by Stone, is mentioned in the second publication as indicating 'that industrial buildings have lives of over sixty years' (p. 90). In the third publication we find it asserted that 'Generally commercial and industrial buildings are not thought to have a life span on average of more than about 60 years. Changes in trading and production methods obviously reduce the life span. In a period of 40 years it is reasonable to expect that two-thirds of the buildings will be redeveloped, and some will be extensively altered in addition. . . . The replacement of two-thirds of [the present total area of factory, retailing, wholesale and office floor-space] might cost around £9000 million' (p.117). Clearly the survey conducted in a single area, enquiring into the lives of assets built in a period that has involved two world wars, and revealing that 62 out of 174 factories were over forty-two years old cannot be taken as evidence to support the assumption that two-thirds of a wider class of buildings will be redeveloped in a period of forty years, but none other is given. The figure of £9000 million must for this and other reasons be treated with some reserve. Many Lancashire cotton mills, now well over sixty years old, still flourish as mills, others have been adapted to new functions.

6. Only some towns had building registers as early as 1860–3, and not all of the early records remain. However, some useful work can be done from the data which exist. See J. Parry Lewis, op. cit. pp. 64–7, 301–25, 334–51. This book also contains some data about demolitions in Liverpool.

7. For a useful summary of work in this field see P. Cowan, 'Depreciation, Obsolescence and Ageing', Joint Unit for Planning Research, 1965, Seminar Paper I (unpublished).

8. Most British work in this field has resulted in only point estimates without any indication of accuracy, as indicated in note 5, above.

9. G. C. F. Capper and J. Parry Lewis, 'Decay, Development and Land Values', in *Manchester School*, XXXII (1964) 25–41, reprinted as a pamphlet of the Civic Trust for the North-West.

10. See Capper and Lewis, op. cit., and Lewis, op. cit. pp. 268 ff.

11. Historical building statistics are scarce. In Britain there has not been a reasonably steady level, or growth, of building for as long a period as this since the earlier available data for 1700 (Lewis, op. cit.). In the U.S.A. there has been no such phenomenon since their data began in the 1830s—see *Historical Statistics of the United States, 1789–1945* (Bureau of the Census; 1945). Canada has had no such phenomenon since its earliest recorded data for 1867—see K. A. H. Buckley, *Capital formation in Canada 1896–1930* (Canadian Studies in Economics 2: Toronto, 1955)—while in Europe there was none in Italy—see

Indagine Statistica sullo svilluppo del reddito hazionale dell'Italia dal 1861 al 1956 (Instituto Centrale di Statistica: Roma, 1957)—or in any of the other countries for which statistics go back early enough. Migration patterns to South America and Australia make it unlikely that these areas have ever had this kind of growth.

12. Briggs, op. cit. pp. 230 and 236. See also K. Feiling, *The Life of Neville Chamberlain* (London, 1946), especially ch. vi, and J. L. Garvin, *The Life of Joseph Chamberlain* I (London, 1932).
13. A. Marshall, *Principles of Economics*, 8th ed. (London, 1947) book IV, ch. x, section 3, p. 273.
14. W. Alonso, *Location and Land Use: toward a general theory of land rent* (Cambridge, Mass., 1964).
15. L. Wingo, *Transportation and Urban Land* (Washington, 1961).
16. For a fuller account of some of the aspects of this concluding remark see J. Parry Lewis, 'The Study of Urban Change', Special University of London Lecture in Estate Management, 1968, reproduced in *Estates Gazette*, 2 and 9 March 1968, and 'The Statistical Study of Urban Change', in *Proceedings of the Manchester Statistical Society*, 1967.

CHAPTER 6

1. This of course ignores the demolition that will already have taken place for a variety of reasons. The upswing between 1865 and some time in the early or mid-seventies was common to most English towns. See J. Parry Lewis, *Building Cycles and Britain's Growth* (London, 1965), especially app. 4.
2. D.E.A., *The North-West: a regional study* (H.M.S.O. London, 1965) p. 75.
3. A. A. Nevitt, *Housing Taxation and Subsidies* (London, 1966).

APPENDIX 5

1. J. H. von Thünen, *Der Isolierte Staat in Beziehung auf Landwirtschaft und National Ökonomie* (Jena, 1921).
2. A. Marshall, *Principles of Economics*, 8th ed. (London, 1947).
3. Ibid. book IV, ch. x, section 3, p. 273.
4. Ibid. book v, ch. xi, section 1, p. 441.
5. This summary of Marshall's views is included as a convenient way of introducing certain ideas, rather than as a prelude to a survey of theory. For this one may, if one is particularly interested in location, consult the works of A. Lösch—*The Economics of Location* (New Haven, Conn., 1954)—and W. Isard—*Location and Space-economy* (New York, Mass., 1956) and *Methods of Regional Analysis* (Cambridge, Mass.,

1960)—while for a general, non-mathematical approach to the wider problems of urban land economics there is a standard work, R. U. Ratcliff, *Urban Land Economics* (New York, 1949). See also W. Alonso, *Location and Land Use: toward a general theory of land rent* (Cambridge, Mass., 1964).

APPENDIX 8

1. *The Changing Use of Land in Britain* (London, 1962) p. 168, table v.

Index